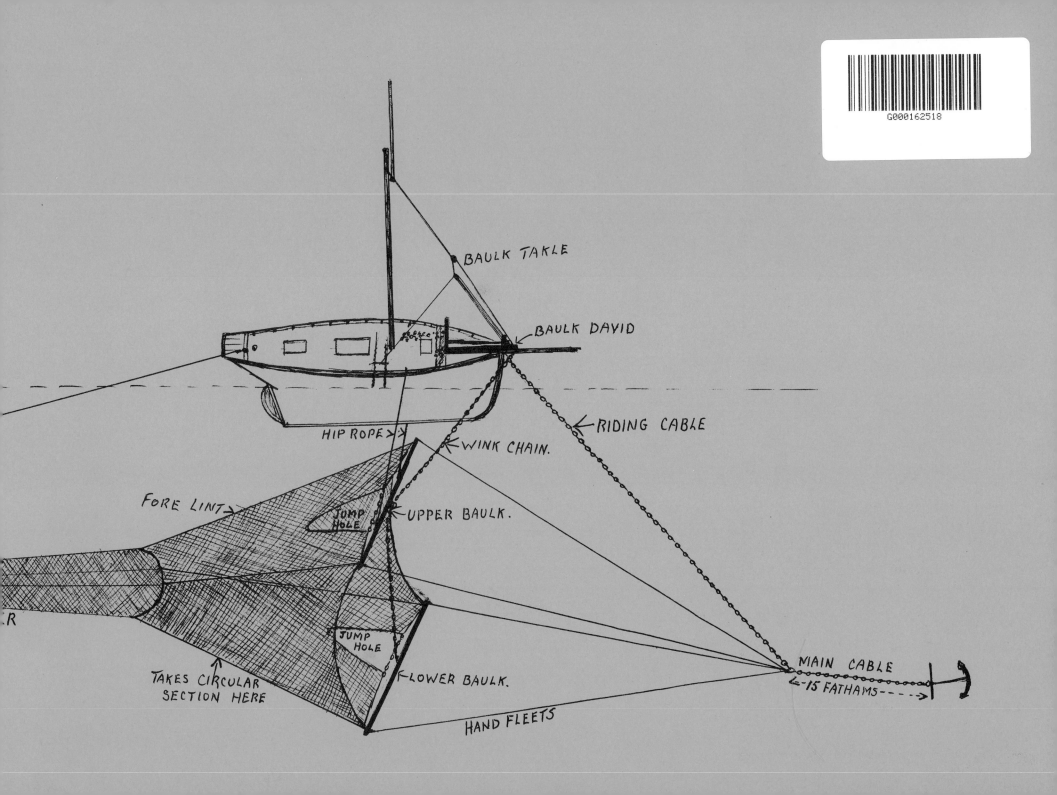

BAULK TAKLE

BAULK DAVID

RIDING CABLE

HIP ROPE

WINK CHAIN.

FORE LINT

JUMP HOLE

UPPER BAULK.

TAKES CIRCULAR SECTION HERE

JUMP HOLE

LOWER BAULK.

MAIN CABLE

←--15 FATHAMS----→

HAND FLEETS

The Stowboaters

With all good wishes

[signature]

November 1997

Stowboating in shallow water. The lower baulk is on the bottom instead of being suspended by the windchain. The upper baulk is clear of the water, snug under the bowsprit, supported to starboard by the baulk tackle and to port by the jib halyard, instead of hanging on the templines. The stringer is shackled in at the outer end of the cable, instead of the inner end. Compare with the usual deepwater setting shown on page 14. The cod end knot, shown in detail on page 18, is distended for clarity; in practice it was tied tightly like a knot in a stocking.

JAMES. DODDS.

The Stowboaters

by Hervey Benham

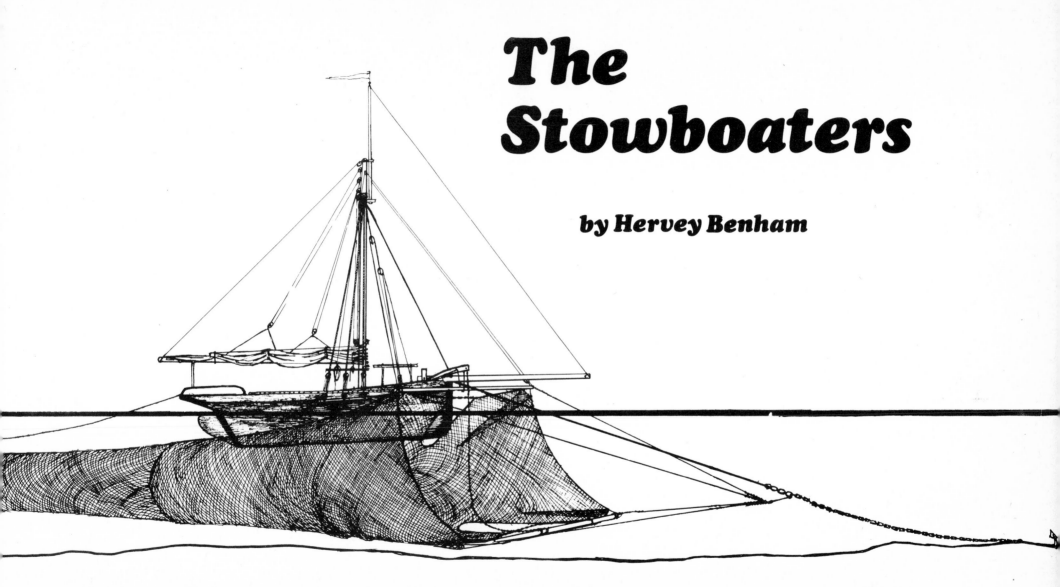

Essex County Newspapers Ltd.

By the same author

Last Stronghold of Sail (Harrap, 1947, out of print).
   Stories of the Colne and Blackwater.

Down Tops'l (Harrap, 1951, reprint 1971).
   The story of the East Coast sailing barges.

Once Upon a Tide (Harrap, 1955, reprint 1971).
   East Coast shipping in the 18th and 19th centuries.

Two Cheers for the Town Hall (Hutchinson, 1964).
   A study of the structure of local public affairs before
   reorganisation, based on Colchester.

Some Essex Watermills (Essex County Newspapers, 1976).
   An account of the mills, past and present, of the rivers
   Chelmer, Blackwater and Colne, and of the Essex
   coastal tidemills.

© Hervey Benham
First published 1977 by Essex County Newspapers Ltd., .,
Colchester.
Format by Mirams Design, Colchester.
Photoset by QB Ltd., Colchester.
Printed by Hewitt Photolith Ltd., Colchester.

ISBN 0 9505944 0 7

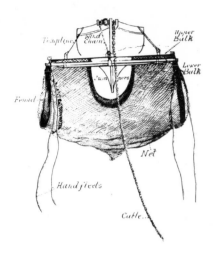
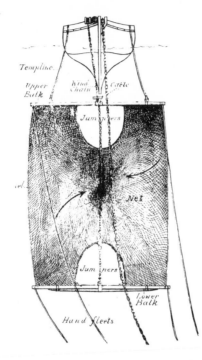

Drawings by the late Dr J Murie of Leigh, showing gear with baulks closed and baulks open. See pages 13 and 41.

Contents

The photographs are by the late Douglas Went of Brightlingsea, with the following exceptions: pages 9 and 46, from the Benton Collection at Essex Record Office; page 22, Nichols; page 30, courtesy of Mr H Wright; page 32, courtesy of Mr D Heard; page 36, Stimson; page 38, courtesy of Southend Chamber of Commerce; page 42, A Pyner; page 44, Beken.

The drawing on page 14 is also available as a poster, size 30 inches by 20 inches, at £1.50 plus 50p packing and postage from James Dodds, Bourne Mill, Colchester.

The stowboat gear offers an interesting opportunity to the model maker. Details from my own somewhat crude attempt, from which arose the interest which led to the writing of this book. On left, the templine should be secured further forward on the rail.

Introduction

THIS BOOK is really the testament of two men, "Navvy" Mussett of Tollesbury and Ken Francis of Brightlingsea. I have been merely their amanuensis in setting down this account of a characterful Thames estuary fishery, which lasted 500 years, had its greatest age in the two places named, and has now passed away in our lifetime.

"Navvy" Mussett is by birth a Mersea man, a member of a Huguenot family numerous on that island. His own branch of it has borne the nickname of "Navvy" back to the eighteenth century; after his time it will pass to his son, and his daughter is sometimes referred to as "the gal Navvy." Until I had to write it down for these pages I had no idea his name was Walter; if it comes to that, I have other friends in Mersea today whose real Christian names I have never known and perhaps never shall.

He moved to Tollesbury (where he says he is still regarded as a "furriner") some thirty years ago, perhaps because the Tollesbury men are (or then were) rovers and the Mersea men (good luck to them!) have always tended to be stay-at-home.

At eighty-two, he can remember the last Revenue cutter in Mersea, and the creeks when they were the home of nearly fifty smacks and only four yachts. He has known every sort of fishing, and gone deep-sea in the Merchant Navy. He was a crack yacht skipper both in the

twelve metres and in the later off-shore champion *Jocasta*, but he was never happier than when enjoying the experiences narrated in these pages.

Even when he was in the navy during the Second World War, escorting the convoys into the Thames estuary, he could not stop fishing. He made a trawl out of gun cotton picked out into six-fathom lengths and seldom came home on leave without a box of fish. At Cliffe, near Chatham, he made a stowboat net and hung it on the pier railings. It caught a ton of sprats and pulled the railings down. "Navvy" converted a fort into a smoke house and had the defaulters string the sprats on wires and collect oak roots from fields being cleared for farming. Sixty men in his unit were issued with new shoes just before Christmas. He told them to bring the empty shoe boxes and filled every one with smoked sprats. "The ones with the biggest feet got the most sprats," he recalls.

Ken Francis, who is seventeen years his junior, comes from a family equally well known in Brightlingsea. He started stowboating with his father Joseph in 1924, just in time for the best years. A member of the old Colne Fishery Company, he has also done plenty of oyster dredging and "culching" (another trade yet to be recorded). After war-time service as Chief Petty Officer, he was for four years with Musson & Co., the oyster merchants, then for six years

"Navvy" Mussett handling enter net out of the cutching vat.

was assistant at Brightlingsea oyster cleansing plant, and in 1955 was appointed head fishery officer for the Kent and Essex Sea Fisheries Committee, a post from which he retired in 1975.

I have also enjoyed the collaboration of two of the last generations of stowboaters, Malcolm MacGregor and Dick Harman, whose contribution is specially valuable, firstly because they introduced me to the memories of their old skipper, Dennis Heard, an outstanding member of one of Tollesbury's greatest families, and secondly because they were able to see that they were involved in a vanishing way of life, which sharpened their awareness, just as the last generation of sailing barge skippers knew that their wonderful craft could not last much

Ken Francis and his father, Joseph Francis.

longer, and appreciated them the more.

Malcolm worked as a boy from 1950 to 1955 with Dennis Heard in the *Charlotte Ellen* (restored as a sailing smack in 1977.) He and his brother, Ian, who went with Basil Steady in the *Alberta*, are thus probably the youngest men to have participated. Dick went in the *Charlotte Ellen* for two winters and both men fell under the spell of the smacks. Malcolm bought the *G & A* at Mersea, had her rebuilt and worked her from 1955 to 1956 when he became foreman of the Colchester Oyster Fishery. Dick bought and rerigged another former stowboater, *A.D.C.*, now perhaps the most splendid smack under sail on the coast, and the pair restarted the Colne Smack Race. With sailing barges and steam craft also now participating, this is organised by Malcolm's wife, Lilian, and has become one of the most delightful events on the coast.

I could not have had better mentors. The errors and omissions are mine; the rich treasury of hitherto unrecorded fishing lore in these chapters is theirs.

The best reward for so much dedicated enthusiasm would be the preservation of a set of stowboat gear, which is still available for the purpose. Its huge proportions would, of course, make any effective display very difficult, and so far the idea has defeated such museums and preservation societies as I have been able to consult. It will, however, be a tragedy if some way is not found, for soon it will be too late.

At Leigh, which for my purpose includes Southend, I have been helped by Ian Young and particularly by John Bridge, a progressive and successful young fisherman who carries on a proud family tradition, and who introduced me to Cecil Osborne, one of the few Leighmen able to recall the old days there.

I have also relied on the work of Dr James Murie (1832-1925) who laboured for many years on a study of the Thames Estuary Sea Fisheries, commissioned by Kent and Essex Sea Fisheries Committee. Only volume one was published, in 1903; a study of Leigh, on the rather curious grounds that it represented "a kind of epitome of most of the topics affecting the working of the seas fisheries' districts generally."

When Dr Murie died twenty-two years later, at the age of ninety-two, a few pages of the next volume were in print, but the old man made a fire outside his cottage of his manuscripts and galley proofs. After his death the charred remains were rescued and painstakingly reconstructed by Mr W Pollitt of Southend Central Library, where the result may still be consulted. On some pages only a few words were legible, so that following the sense is not always easy. Dr

Murie was described* as "industrious and dilatory, broadminded and opinionative, and disposed to present the side of his character most opposed to the views of those under whom he had to work." He was not afraid to turn out at three o'clock in the morning to see fishing methods for himself, but like many other interpreters (including no doubt myself) he was sometimes confused by the task of comprehending puzzling processes and describing them in words and pictures.

Among published sources I have used E W H Holdsworth's *Sea Fisheries of Great Britain and Ireland* and *Apparatus for Fishing* (1883) and *An Account of the Fishing Gear of England and Wales* by F M Davis (Ministry of Agriculture, Fisheries and Food, Fisheries Investigation Series II, Vol 21, No 8, HMSO 1923, updated in 1959).

I am also indebted to John Leather, whose *Gaff Rig* contains information on the south coast sprat fisheries and the best account of the Essex stowboating smacks, and whose *The Northseamen* opens with the best account of a stowboating voyage.

The Solent stowboaters are described, briefly but attractively, by R C Leslie in *A Sea Painter's Log*, and Clodd's *Aldeburgh* deals with the fishery there. Edgar March's *Inshore Craft of Britain* (Vol I) has some information particularly from Gravesend as well as reproducing Murie's incomprehensible drawings of bawleys with the anchor chain over the starboard bow. Some good personal memories of Hazell White, of Brightlingsea, appeared in the *East Coast Digest*, April, 1977, while this book was in the press.

* Sir Peter Chalmers-Mitchell, in the centenary history of the Zoological Society of London, 1929.

For details of the trade at Brightlingsea I am indebted to Mr John Fieldgate.

At Wivenhoe I have been helped particularly by Mr Lewis Worsp and Mr C F Woodward, at King's Lynn by Mr H J Castleton and in Lancashire by Mr Alan Lockett of Barrow-in-Furness.

I have been particularly fortunate over illustrations. That great photographer, the late Douglas Went of Brightlingsea, recorded the smacks in winter as well as the yachts in summer; these photos are almost all examples of his art. The drawings are by an artist of the younger generation, James Dodds, who is also a qualified shipwright with experience of sailing aboard at least one former stowboater, the *Shamrock*, which he helped to sail to Exmouth, her present home. He has joined me in the original research and used all his skills in describing almost forgotten techniques in pictures, a task in some ways more demanding than mine in recording them in words.

Finally I am once again grateful to Mrs Eileen Upsher and Mrs Sandra Hopwood for their unsparing patience in typing and preparing these pages for the press.

Hervey Benham
Feldy
The Lane
West Mersea 1977

CHAPTER ONE

'The Minims of the Sea'

THE STORY of the most characterful fishery of the Thames estuary begins with a decision that was intended to be the end of it.

In 1488 Parliament observed that "in late days for a singular covertise and lucre ... certain persons have been used to set and ordain certain boats called stall boats, fastened with ankers, having with them such manner of unreasonable nets and ingines that all manner of fry and brood ... is taken and destroyed as well as great fishes unseasonable, as the said persons in part feed their hogges, and the residue they put and lay it in pitts in the ground, which else would turn to such perilous infection of air that no person thither resorting should it abide and suffer."

This declamatory denunciation went on to offer a reward of £10 to informers, but even so it is doubtful if the prohibition was effective. It has been the custom of English officialdom to recognise any innovation by an attempt to suppress it; a century before, the first trawls had been similarly condemned. So the stowboat was at this time either newly devised or growing in size or numbers sufficiently to attract attention.

The Act quoted was made perpetual in 1491, but it was either repealed or disregarded, for in 1547 stallboatmen from Harwich, Maldon, St Osyth, East Mersea, Fingringhoe and Colchester were ordered to be arrested for failure to pay dues to the Rector of King's Chapel in the Tower of London, presumably for unloading at or near the Tower. Brightlingsea, the great centre of later days, is not mentioned (possibly because

A good sample of "Wallet whoppers".

its fishermen had paid), and the trade declined in importance at Harwich, but otherwise these were the stowboaters' villages for the ensuing centuries, with Tollesbury taking it up for the last half century.

Soon after this, in 1558, an Act was passed "for the preservation of spawn and fry which heretofore hath been destroyed in rivers and streams salt and freshe within this Realme inasmuch that in divers places they feed Swynes and Dogges with the fry and spawn of fishe and otherwise (lamentable and horrible to be reported) destroys the same to the great hynderance and decaye of the Commonwealthe."

The language of the Elizabethan legislators may sound laughably histrionic, and the

attempt to ban all catching other than for human consumption was probably an indefensible oppression of fishermen and in the end a waste of fish. Yet the instinct was right, for in the age of the second Elizabeth the cattle of Europe are fed on fish meal which is recommended for domestic pets in the yet more hysterical language of the TV commercial — and the North Sea has been almost swept bare of fish. These rich and shallow waters would always have served to feed the people of Europe; to expect them also to feed their livestock proved too much.

Since the sixteenth century, records are scantier and it is difficult to see how or why the old name stallboat (meaning fixed) evolved into stowboat (with its suggestion of stowage). The meaning may be that the fishing was done with sails stowed, but it does not seem a natural transition and I suspect there is an explanation to be discovered, as for several of the technical terms used. The first instinct in maritime mysteries is to seek a Dutch connection, but this I have not succeeded in tracing*.

The opposition was probably principally from the herring fishery, for it was commonly believed that sprats are the young of herring, though in fact they are a distinct species. Tobias Gentleman, a Yarmouth mariner, complained in 1614 that "the men of Colnewater from St

*At Harwich in the nineteenth century the craft lying in the harbour to receive and store cod were referred to as stowboats or stovets. Again this reference could be either to the fact they were anchored or that they were used for stowage.

Andrew [November 30] until Candlemas [February 2] and sometimes longer, do set forth stallboats amongst the sands of the Theames mouth for to take sprats with great stall nets with a great poake; and they standing in the Swin or the Kings Channell, on the back of the Gunfleate, do there take, instead of sprats, infinite thousands of young Herrings, smaller than sprats and not good to be eaten . . . [yet] they do fill the bushell at Billingsgate, where they do sell them for sprats . . . sometimes at twopence a peck. If they were allowed to live till mid-summer they would be fat herrings worth twenty shillings or thirty shillings a barrell." A price of twopence a peck would mean eightpence a bushel — a good price for those days.

Half a century later, in 1662, Thomas Fuller in his *Worthies of England* observed: "These are sprats, caught hereabouts and brought hither [Colchester] in incredible abundance whereon the poor weavers (numerous in the city) make much of their repast, cutting rands [meat between the flank and the rump], rumps, sirloins, chines, and all joints of beef out of them as lasting in season well nigh a quarter of a year. They are the minims of the sea; and their cheapness is the worst thing (well considered the best) which can be said of them. Were they as dear they would be as toothsome (being altogether as wholesome) as anchovies, for then their price would give a gust unto them in the judgement of palate men."

No doubt the thousands of poor weavers and their equally hungry fellow workers put away a good many bushels, and no doubt their families were sick of sprats by Christmas, for while there is nothing tastier than the occasional meal the penetrating oily smell of their continual cooking must have added to the stench inseparable from

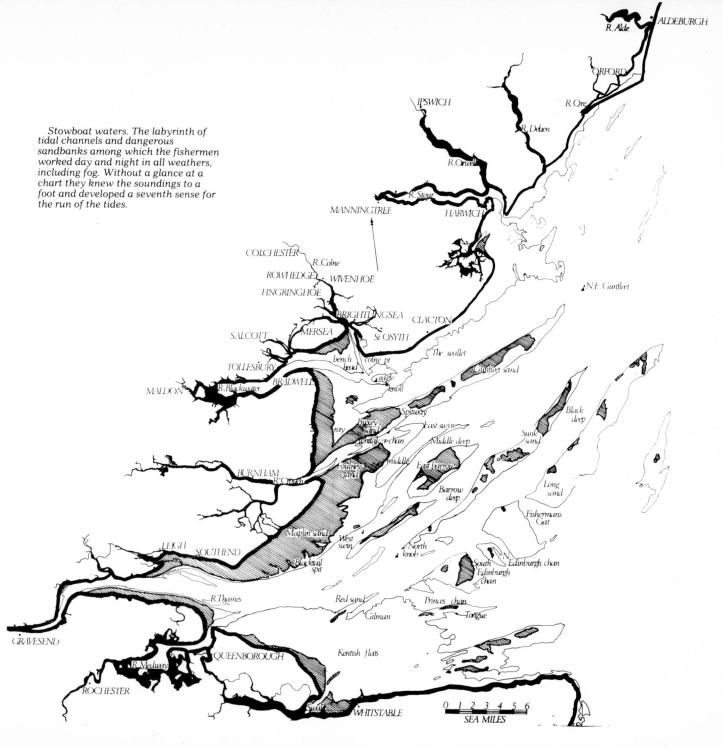

Stowboat waters. The labyrinth of tidal channels and dangerous sandbanks among which the fishermen worked day and night in all weathers, including fog. Without a glance at a chart they knew the soundings to a foot and developed a seventh sense for the run of the tides.

5

The gulls wheel over the loaded smacks in Brightlingsea Creek on a misty winter's morning. A scene from the 1920s before the time of auxiliary engines, for the smacks still have their gaff mainsails.

Below: The creek in a different mood. Such bitter winters were commoner half a century ago than today. Sheet ice, carried by a strong tide, could cut deep into the wooden smacks' waterlines.

this important but dirty cottage industry. There is no record of preserving or exporting at this time and once this local trade was satisfied it must be assumed that the early fishing was largely for manure. A Colchester man had a stallboat filled with manure at the Hythe round the time of the original prohibition of 1488.

There are few accounts from the seventeenth and eighteenth centuries, if only because by this time the trade must have been accepted and taken for granted, and chroniclers have the irritating habit of failing to observe the familiar, in addition to a preference for doing their sightseeing in summer. Fishing boats and coastal traders were only gradually evolving into separate classes, and no doubt the doggers and crayers of medieval and Tudor times, and the eighteenth century smacks and sloops, were fitted out in good seasons with "unreasonable engines" and stood in the channels and fairways watching the barks and hoys sail past and glad to see the clumsy collier cats and brigs go clear.

With the nineteenth century, Government commissions and reports tell of a steady and regular trade. Seasons were always erratic, but there seems no evidence that the overall balance between plenty and scarcity varied greatly till the disastrous over-fishing of modern times. In 1836 the number of stowboaters was put at between 400 and 500. Witnesses before a commission in 1878 varied between those who said that on five-year averages there had been no difference over forty years, and those who detected that decline which is an almost invariable fisherman's view in any age. Nor have the seasons, from early November to the beginning of February, varied in 500 years, though with the change from an ecclesiastical to a secular calendar it has become customary to associate the opening with the Lord Mayor of London's Day (November 9) instead of St Andrew's Day (November 30).

The earliest that sprats were ever known to come in any quantity in living memory was November 5. The day, in 1934, is recalled by Ken Francis, for he and his brother Jack had the *Ellen* already fitted out and were filling in time dredging oysters for the Colne Fishery Company. Early that morning a barge skipper sang out that there were clouds of gulls under the Buxey. The Colne company foreman released them at twelve o'clock and they steamed straight to the North Buxey Buoy, shooting the gear 200 yards from the cloud of gulls. Within half an hour the net was full and floating on the surface. They filled the hold, let the rest go and were anchored in the creek by six o'clock.

By 1866 the dimensions of the stowboat net mouth, which have varied little since, were already established. And by this time, too, there had started a century of vigour and enterprise on Colneside.

From the villages of this estuary came three generations of bold and ambitious mariners who, as yachtsmen in summer and fishermen in winter, were second to none in the British Isles, and to satisfy their needs and aspirations there evolved fleets of smacks which likewise feared no comparison with any in the world. Whether the racing yachts produced the smacks or the skill of the smacksmen was the making of the yachts is a question as open as that of the chicken and the egg; in fact it was perhaps the brilliance of the creative Colneside shipbuilders, Sainty and Harvey, which gave the district its greatest age.

The first class Colne smacks were of twenty to fifty tons, around sixty-five feet long, with fifteen feet beam. The main boom was around forty-five feet long and the bowsprit was twenty-five feet outboard. These smacks would land 1,000 bushels of sprats as well as dredging deep-sea oysters off Terschelling and scallops down channel, working for oysters down to the Channel Islands and to the Forth and round Land's End to Ireland, Wales and the Solway. This fleet numbered 132 in 1874, but few survived the First World War.

The second class smacks were of fifteen to twenty tons, loading 300 bushels. The third class smacks, of around ten tons and under, were chiefly confined to local oyster dredging, with some fish trawling and winkling.

These were the craft which saw the final phase of stowboating. In the summer many of them were laid up in mud berths, their owners away making the grand tour of the regatta circuit in search of prize money, and maybe dreaming, as they slummed it in the overcrowded foc's'les of these otherwise palatial sailing machines, of the carefree winter days ahead.

Tollesbury was later in awakening, for stowboating did not start there till around 1890*.

At this time, when the eighteen-ton smacks were becoming more profitable than the big Colne thirty-tonners, Tollesbury came to have more in common with Brightlingsea, Wivenhoe and Rowhedge than with its less enterprising Blackwater neighbours, Maldon and West Mersea.

Even so, Tollesbury retained its own char-

* This was stated by Alf Drake to Dennis Heard. And Ken Francis recalls Brightlingsea men saying to Tollesbury men, "We taught you stowboating and now you take the bread out of our mouths."

Loaded stowboater running into Brightlingsea Creek in a breeze.

acter and style. For example, when the smacks housed their summer top masts in a breeze (and they seldom sailed with bare top mast, as so many of the "Old Gaffers" do in today's revival), the Colnemen always took out a leg from the top mast rigging, but this the Tollesbury men did not have, preferring to coil up the wire under the crosstrees — a feature by which they could be recognised. And while the place may have been the last to adopt stowboating it was to retain the old practices, including hand-netting of gear by the men and their womenfolk ashore, right into the 1950's. This was because Tollesbury was so isolated that it was less subject to outside influence and offered less in the way of alternative occupations.

The last generation of Colne and Tollesbury fishermen, grandsons often of the men who built their smacks, survived to see the best days of all, between the wars, when at last pickling yards and canning factories made some economic sense of the market and only the surplus went for manure. Between 1923 and 1938 Brightling-sea, the centre of the trade, presented a never-to-be-forgotten scene all through the winter, as busy with sprats as were Lowestoft and Yar-mouth with herring, the creek full of beautiful cutters, loaded so their decks were nearly in the water, their great nets festooned from their masts, the big skiffs constantly coming and

going as they were sculled to the yards and lighters, stacked high with barrels, full or empty. Ken Francis recalls twenty-six smacks lying together in Brightlingsea Creek, fully laden, with 350 to 450 bushels in each*.

Catches might be made anywhere in the Thames estuary. Sometimes it was necessary to sail across to the Kent shore; occasionally the smacks had only to move half a mile from their moorings. Migrating shoals struck the east coast simultaneously with the herring, arriving at Southwold and Aldeburgh in October, and

working their way southwards. Sometimes they seemed to enter the Thames estuary through the Swin, sometimes by the more southerly channels; around the turn of the century it was considered that a northerly approach meant "there are bound to be a lot of fish."*

It was a fishery which demanded all the inherited skill of generations of Thames estuary skippers. Often with three or four families to support, the smacks had to work, and could not wait for favourable conditions. Day and night were all the same; sleep was not considered, and was only missed when both watches had to stand to.

The dawn and dusk lulls in the wind were used, and if the weather was very unsettled a smack would lie to under the sand to put in for the ebb, as this meant getting the net at low water under safer conditions. Sometimes the only chance was to put in at low water, committing the smack to riding out the whole of the flood with the prospect of a dangerous cut in at high water. If it blew up on the flood, as it so often did, the skipper would be in the strange position of praying that he was not getting too many fish.

Fog meant calm weather, and a lot of work was done when you could not see three boats' lengths ahead, specially when motors made such getting about possible. Dick Harman recalls as the most memorable experience of his life three trips on successive days in the *Charlotte Ellen* from Wivenhoe to the North Red Sand, the weather "thick as guts and freezing with it." The navigation was at full speed all the way, straight off the clock on to the lead. No notice was taken of fairway buoys other than to avoid hitting them; the whole

Stowboaters in summer. Elise, Sunbeam *and* Xanthe *racing. In accordance with the rule, they carry their beam trawls on deck.*

*A list of the smacks remembered by the contributors to this book appears as an appendix.

*See also Chapter 4.

At Tollesbury. Below: The fleet laid up in summer, with their owners and skippers away yachting. Right: The ADC fitting out.

course was set through racing tides by some instinctive map of the bottom in Dennis Heard's mind.

Reaching their fishing ground the stowboats charged straight into channels busy with groping shipping, rounded up to their anchors and started a furious carillon of fog bells. The answer from the steamers was the rumbling and splashing of their big anchors. Mercifully they swung without collision, but when it came clear what a sight the Barrow presented!

At night the Brightlingsea and Tollesbury craft disdained navigation lights; in fact the Leighmen could be picked out by their use when the fleets were fishing together in the south channels. A good riding light was thought enough, even when under weigh, and when Tilley lamps came in one of these, hung under the boom, lit the deck and served further to

confuse any threatening shipping! Before 1914 one could look out from Clacton, where the only light visible was in the railway signal box, and see the Wallet looking like a town, gleaming with the lights of the stowboaters. Today the seas are deserted at night and even villages have to be polluted with festoons of yellow illumination, lit up like a lunatic's funfair*.

It was a noble and adventurous life, but it was also a hard and cruel one. Dennis Heard, though he occasionally went yachting, lived the life of an all-the-year round skipper-owner, spending the summer shrimping and dredging. This

*Navigation by telephone kiosk was quite a feature of the 1920s and 1930s in waters neglected by Trinity House. The only lights at the entrance of the Colne were those on a wreck on East Mersea Stone, and in a kiosk near Bateman's Tower, while to find Mersea Quarters the illuminated telephone kiosk near the Victory Inn could be seen from the North-West Knoll.

Fitting out at Brightlingsea.

Above: Hugh Brand painting the Favourite, *with Joseph Francis'* Ellen *on left.*

Right: Ron Death painting the Cobham. *Behind is the former Lowestoft drifter PAG, fitting out for scalloping. She was nicknamed* Pork and Greens, *with various unprintable alternatives.*

meant that in addition to his stowboat gear he had to keep up three different kinds of dredge rigging for culch, for five fingers, and for brood oysters, as well as his shrimp trawls, of which he had no fewer than seven. He was netting every minute of the time the smack was brought up, day and night, except for a few hours' sleep — and he kept a ball of twine in his bunk so that when he woke up it reminded him to turn out. His way of life gave him time for nothing but nets — and he considered he had it easy because his father made his own sails.

You may read in Brightlingsea church the tablets which record how "Charles Barber, age 46, Perished with his Smack *Greyhound* through collision in the Swin, September 3, 1884", and how "Theodore Barber, Age 16, Perished with his Father". Dick Harman's father's mother was their close relative, and though he was brought up among the big thousand-bushel smacks and knew a lot about them he refused to talk of them beyond observing that they had drowned half his family and starved the other half.

Mersea and Maldon men, along with those of the Crouch and Roach, evolved a different life-style, preferring to stay at home and work all the year round on their abundant oysters and winkles, with some fish trawling in season. Thus, they had neither large enough craft nor a sufficiently adventurous outlook for stowboating, and the only boats which took part from Mersea were the *George and Alice* and the *Priscilla*, which was cut in half and lengthened for the purpose. Some of the Harwich "cod bangers" joined in to a small extent, probably as their traditional fisheries in Iceland and on the Dogger were taken from them by steam trawlers. These included the ketch-rigged well smacks *Test* and *Vestal* (owned by Alexander)

and the former pilot cutter *Volunteer*. According to an old Harwich fisherman*: "The *Volunteer* was sometimes a cutter and sometimes a yawl. When she was a stow, that is when she was going stovetting for sprats, she was yawl rigged; when she went down channel dredging for oysters and scallops she was cutter rigged, the owner having two separate sets of sails and spars."

The trade was carried on by at least one smaller craft in the 1840s, for when the newly elected MP for Harwich was unseated for corruption in 1847 one of those he had bribed was Edward Saxby, a fisherman whose boat had been seized for debt. Saxby, who got the boat back by selling his vote, used her for whelking, cement stone dredging and "stoperting", and said he could earn £100 for sprats in a good season. In recent years the only Harwich participant was the *Corsair*.

In Suffolk sprats were as important to Aldeburgh in Elizabethan times as they were to become at Brightlingsea 250 years later, for catches by 300 mariners were said to amount to 30,000 lasts (which would be over thirty million fish) in the annual winter "spratte fare". Most of these were probably taken at sea by drifters, but stowboats were used in the river, often anchored for days on end in the Gull, or in the main channel by the southern tip of Havergate Island. They are shown in a map of 1588 and were blamed for obstruction of the channel and for destruction of fish. Ely Abbey and the Lord of the Manor jointly charged ten shillings a year

*Mr Nettlingham, talking to the late Dr J L Groom. In his invaluable unpublished researches into the Harwich fisheries, Dr Groom constantly uses the form stovet and stovetting. This could be a mishearing, but Dr Groom was meticulous over such points of detail and I conclude it was a Harwich usage.

for a stallboat's right to fish in the Gull, and, to preserve this revenue, saw to it that they did not fish outside in the bay.

Blowe's *Travels* (1673) notes: "At mid-winter Aldeburgh for sprats, it being the only place in England for drying or redding of sprats." "Red" or smoked sprats were long an Aldeburgh speciality; Defoe in 1822 quipped: "In their own language they make red sprats or in English they make sprats red."

Further evidence that stowboats were used at sea at the end of the eighteenth century is provided by a Lowestoft witness*, who declared: "From 150 to 200 boats are employed on the coast stowboating and sprat fishing. In old days there used to be a great many soles, now we have none. This is attributed to the stowboats."

By 1819 it was noted* that: "The sprat fishery to which in former times Aldeburgh owed all its prosperity is now nearly done away." In fact it goes on to this day, but the Aldeburgh men have come to concentrate exclusively on drift netting off the shore, and with the drifters securing prime fish the stowboaters' catches must have been chiefly for manure.

The Kentish men at Deal and Dover also favoured drift nets and did not use stowboats. The obvious reason is that the sandbanks of the estuary make narrow channels unsuitable for drift nets, particularly as most of them are busy with shipping, and they also concentrate the shoals to the benefit of the stowboats. But it is curious that even in the Wallet, Colne and

*Mr B Brown, quoted by Nall: *Chapters on the East Anglian Coast.*

*Rev J Ford: *Aldeburgh Described.*

The fleet in Brightlingsea Creek in the 1930s. From left are SWH, Sunbeam, My Alice, AEFA *and* Marion. *Infuenced by the introduction of Bermuda rig in yachts,* AEFA *at this time sported a lofty pole mast, and set a triangular mainsail on it.*

Blackwater, where drift nets are used for herring, they prove unsuccessful for sprats. Drifted sprats being bigger have always found favour for the table, but the catches are much smaller. In 1911, forty-five per cent of the total East Coast catch (1,430 tons) was landed at Brightlingsea: in the heyday of the 1920's and 1930's the town handled eighty per cent of British landings.

At Leigh, Gravesend and up the Medway stowboating was done for whitebait as well as sprats. Outside the Thames estuary the biggest stowboat fishery was in the Solent, and some was also done in the Wash and in Morecambe Bay.

CHAPTER TWO

'The Greate Poake'

THE STOWBOAT net and its gear were unique in elaborate complexity. They parallel the rig of the spritsail sailing barge, perhaps because both were designed, or evolved, to perform the impossible — the sailing barge to enable two men to take 150 tons of cargo up a farmer's creek or across the North Sea, the stowboater to set a marine trap capable of snaring ten tons of fish without mechanical aid.

The topsail barge, while of ancient lineage, was essentially a creation of nineteenth century ingenuity. The stowboater's gear may have been perfected and developed in size during this time, but its basic principles are probably ancient, if only because its various parts have their own names, the derivations of which are in some cases no longer understood.

The fishing boat lay at anchor with her net rigged below her. The net was extended by two baulks, of which the lower was weighted, and these baulks were controlled by the handfleets, which were attached to the anchor cable by a short length of wire or chain, the stringer. There was also a fathom or so of chain between the handfleets and the baulks. This was looped neatly over the baulks to prevent the handfleets

getting foul turns. The handfleets were fifteen to twenty fathoms long, with the upper pair a fathom longer than the lower pair.

A stowboat anchor weighed up to four cwt. To this was permanently attached three fathoms of heavy chain to which, for ordinary working purposes, the anchor chain was shackled. For stowboating. in the days of sail, this chain was unshackled and a cable shackled on. (The permanent three fathoms were necessary to hold two turns on the windlass and bring the shackle free on deck.)

This cable was some twenty-five fathoms long, according to "Navvy" Mussett, or fifteen fathoms according to Ken Francis, about six inches in circumference with one-inch bass rope wormed into the lay and seized at every fathom. Three or four big links were let into the cable at each end. In deep water the handfleets were shackled to the links at the inboard end of the cable so that when the necessary fifteen fathoms of chain were veered to bring the weight on the handfleets the smack was lying to three fathoms of heavy chain, fifteen or twenty-five fathoms of cable and fifteen fathoms of chain, some forty fathoms in all. In

shallow water the handfleets were shackled to the links at the outboard end of the cable and the smack lay to fifteen fathoms of cable and three fathoms of heavy chain, the working anchor chain not being used.

The cable eased the strain on the smack lying in a sea-way. It was spliced into the links by passing two strands down through the first link and the third up between them. The strands were worked up and down through a few links and seized at each crossing. In addition, short lengths of two-inch rope, the tailings, were short-spliced into the worming ropes at one end and eye-spliced into the first link at the other, the short splices being staggered to avoid a clumsy bulge. The whole join was parcelled in canvas, served and dipped in hot tar. At the end of each season the cable and tailings were cut with an axle close to the first link, and the join remade, so that the cable grew a little shorter each year of its life, which was about five years.

When out of use the baulks were picked up by the baulk tackle and stowed outside the starboard rigging. In the fishing position the upper baulk hung from the templines and the weighted lower baulk was eased down by the

The stowboater's arrangement of anchor chain, anchor cable and short length of chain at the anchor. The large links into which the ends of the cable were worked are exaggerated in size for clarity.

Handfleets shackle here for fishing in deep water

Handfleets shackle here for fishing in shallow water

FATHOM

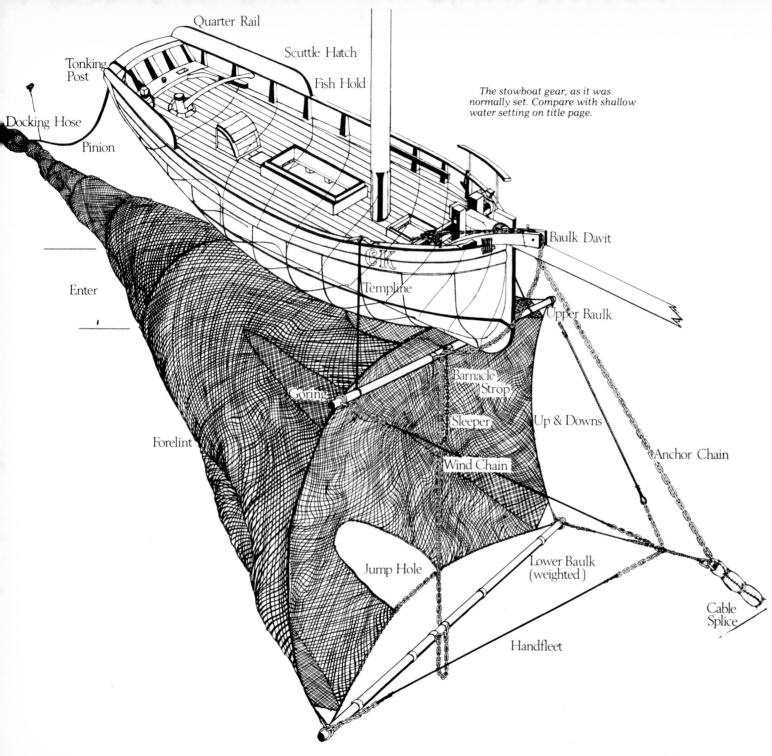

Quarter Rail

Scuttle Hatch

Fish Hold

Tonking Post

Docking Hose

Pinion

The stowboat gear, as it was normally set. Compare with shallow water setting on title page.

Enter

Baulk Davit

Templine

Upper Baulk

Goring

Barnacle Strop

Forelint

Sleeper

Up & Downs

Wind Chain

Anchor Chain

Jump Hole

Lower Baulk (weighted)

Cable Splice

Handfleet

windchain till its weight came on the up-and-downs, ropes to which the sides of the forelint were laced. The windchain led from the windlass over a sheave in the end of the baulk davit, a curved timber projecting over the starboard bow, and through a barnacle strop in the centre of the upper baulk. The inboard end of the baulk davit terminated in an iron fitting inserted in a ring on the deck, or alternatively was bolted through the heel of the bitts.

A toggle on about three feet of light chain, the sleeper, was shackled into the chain about five and a half fathoms from the lower baulk so as to stop the chain riding up and down through the barnacle strop as the smack pitched and keeping the crew awake at night (hence the name). It was the boy's job to pass the sleeper three times round the windlass as the chain was veered, or hauled, and to guide it over the baulk davit.

The usual length of the baulks was twenty-one feet for the upper and twenty-two feet for the lower, the extra foot being to allow a projection which avoided getting a turn of the handfleets round its ends. These dimensions were given by Holdsworth in 1883 and by "Navvy" Mussett in 1976.

Bigger smacks used longer baulks; for eighteen-tonners such as the *Charlotte Ellen*, twenty-five and twenty-six feet were usual, five inch diameter*. The limiting factor was the distance between the after rigging and the smack's stem, for the forward end of the baulks had to pass between the stem and the anchor cable as they hung in the baulk tackle, which

*This is recalled by Dennis Heard. Ken Francis and "Navvy" Mussett considered that twenty-two feet and twenty-three feet were the maximum, with a six-fathom depth.

meant that a twenty-six feet baulk needed thirteen feet clearance*.

The aim was to use gear big enough for one catch to fill the hold without getting fish in the enter. Once the maximum "gape" was achieved this depended on the number of sleeves used, for wider sleeves could not have been cut in or handled by the girdlines. The old class one smacks could not, however, load a thousand bushels in one tide and reckoned on two tides' work at best. With this in mind they often fished at the Tongue, where the tide goes round in a circle, permitting the smack to swing without her gear fouling her anchor.

The net was laced at the sides to the up-and-downs, which were five fathoms, to give a thirty foot "gape", and at the top and bottom to chip ropes which were secured to the baulks. Round spaces known as jump holes were cut out of the centre of the net below the upper and above the lower baulk to save damage to the net from the smack's forefoot. Square stem smacks like the *Shamrock* were difficult for this purpose; round bows as on *Bluebell* and *My Alice* were easier. The baulks were iron-banded against chafe in way of both the windchain and the anchor chain. In the way of the jump holes, about eight feet of quarter-inch chain was spliced into each chip rope.

The net weighed up to a quarter of a ton, and comprised, counting aft from the baulks, fifteen yards of forelint (which thus ended about level with the smack's stern), fifteen yards of entry

*This distance is in fact just thirteen feet in the eighteen-ton *A.D.C.*, but to give a working clearance this would have limited her to say, twenty-four foot baulks maximum. The *Sunbeam* and *Maria* were very long in the head, with the mast stepped very far aft, suggesting that this may have been in mind when they were built.

net or "enter", then three sleeves of finer mesh, each fifteen yards, and finally eight to twelve feet of docking hose of wider mesh, a total length of eighty yards. This huge trap had no pockets or tunnels of any kind.

In making the net the taper was a half mesh in fourteen meshes down the panels of the forelint and enter, which were rectangular. According to "Navvy" Mussett, towards the end of the enter the mesh changed two to one to reduce to herring scale, but according to Ken Francis the whole enter had to be sprat mesh to avoid "thrumming". The sleeves were 200 meshes round ("Navvy" Mussett used 220, which he found easier) and in joining them together it was important to leave the lacings slack. With a tight lacing the fish would not run down from sleeve to sleeve, and the lacings had sometimes to be drawn to clear an overfilled net.

The net took particular strain at the ends of the baulks. The usual practice was to "waste" ten double-netted meshes here, both on the vertical and horizontal panels, by tying in the meshes. These were known as the hundreds; as there were eight such corners a dozen meshes "wasted" at each would in fact make ninety-six. "Navvy" Mussett preferred to net up triangular panels or gorings extending about eight feet deep. These had the additional advantage that they could be replaced when the net began to rot, which was specially likely at the after end of the baulks when the gear was left stowed on deck all winter. The nets were preserved with cutch, to which horse fat or Stockholm tar was added in the boiling coppers. At Brightlingsea they were cut from the ropes at the end of the season and cutched in Sadler's vats in the tan yard where he dressed his barge sails. They were usually hand netted, though Joseph Francis

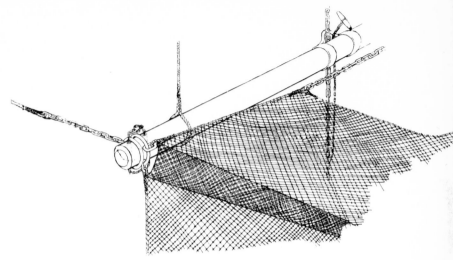

Port end of upper baulk showing goring in net (the hundreds), method of attaching up-and-down and handfleet on short leg of chain, templine spliced round, chip rope and jump hole, and windchain with sleeper toggle about to engage in barnacle strop.

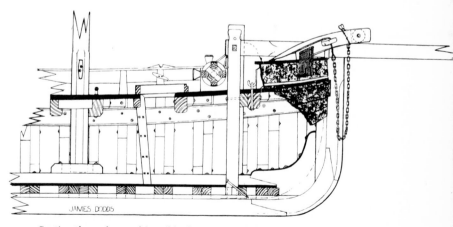

Section through smack's sail locker showing baulk davit seized into rail with wire, its heel secured in an eye bolt through a deck beam. Sometimes the davit was bolted through the bitts. The chain garping strop hangs from the davit with an eye above in which to hook the baulk tackle.

bought and cut made net. He liked to cut the forward score of meshes from the forelint and replace these each year. Double meshing at each score was helpful for this, as well as for strength and for showing the run of the net for mending tears.

In shooting the gear the smack anchored, and the baulks were lowered into the water by the baulk tackle so that they lay along the smack's starboard side, forward. Then the port templine was passed under the anchor chain so that a good pull on it would help with getting the baulks round the bow "aforehead", and the smack was given a sheer to port to open up the cable from the bow. This enabled the baulk ends to pass under the cable, where they were hove up snug under the baulk davit by the windchain, the baulk tackle being let go. Care had to be taken that the baulks were on the aft side of the anchor cable and that they did not dip deep enough for a strong tide to take charge.

Now the handfleets were shackled to the stringer over the port bow, and enough chain veered to tighten the handfleets and pull the baulks clear of the bow. To get this just right the chain was marked with a chain shackle or with white paint at a point which must be on the windlass.

Next the top baulk was girdled by a stopper, made fast to the bitts over the starboard bow, or

SHOOTING THE GEAR

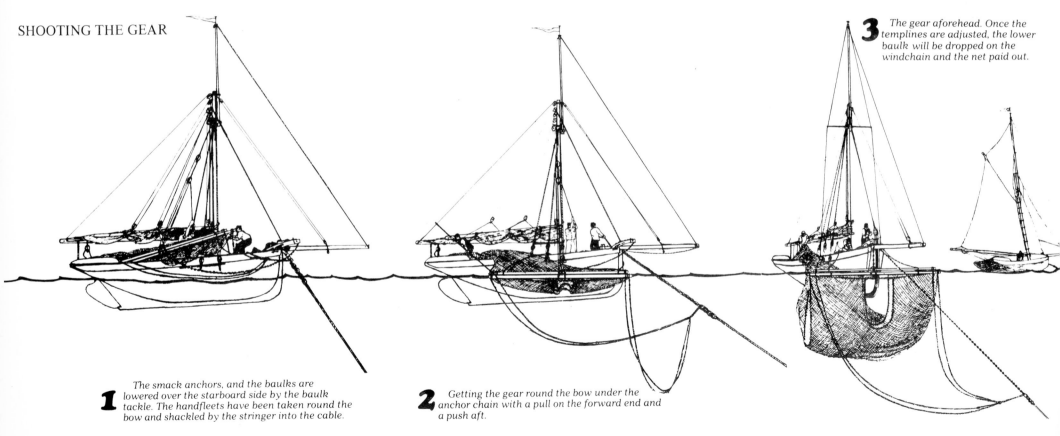

3 *The gear aforehead. Once the templines are adjusted, the lower baulk will be dropped on the windchain and the net paid out.*

1 *The smack anchors, and the baulks are lowered over the starboard side by the baulk tackle. The handfleets have been taken round the bow and shackled by the stringer into the cable.*

2 *Getting the gear round the bow under the anchor chain with a pull on the forward end and a push aft.*

16

by a "garping strop" on the davit, so that the lower baulk could be eased away a little, ensuring it was clear to let fly later.

The forelint was now paid out over the side with a stopper on the enter and the sleeves laid out so they could be easily shot along with the pinion.

With the templines made fast at the depth selected for fishing, the smack was sheered to starboard and the lower baulk was let go, followed by the top baulk which had been

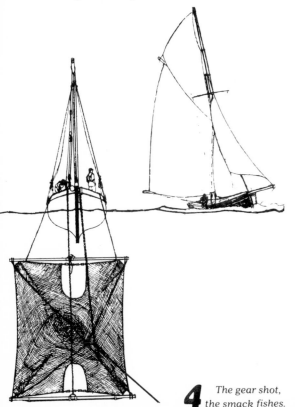

4 *The gear shot, the smack fishes.*

momentarily held on its stopper. While this was being done the stopper on the enter was let go and the sleeves passed quickly over the side. As soon as everything was overboard the sheer was taken off to let the smack straighten up and settle down over her gear. At night one further job remained before the hands off watch could go below — to pull down two reefs in the mainsail, in case the wind piped up before it was time to get the gear.

The reason for marking the chain was that exactly the right amount had to be let go. If too much was veered the weight on the handfleets could break the upper baulk, and if too little was given, the smack's forefoot could slam down on it with the same result. A broken top baulk was capable of staving in the smack's bottom. Another danger was the breaking of the stringer. If this occurred with the baulks under the smack it was necessary to veer sufficient windchain and templines to allow the baulks to clear the stern where they would be made fast till the tide eased.

A cod end buoy was used to help stream the net in slack tides and to prevent it sinking, rigged on a short rope tail attached by a rolling hitch to the pinion, which led from the end of the sleeve to the smack's deck, where it was belayed on the tonking post (as it was called at Tollesbury) or the timber nogging (as the Brightlingsea men called it). This was a wooden upright socketing in a hole in the smack's stern bench which crossed her deck aft of the rudder post. The boom crutch shipped in the port hole; the tonking post or timber nogging in the corresponding hole to starboard.

The fisherman took a pull on the pinion to check the weight of fish in his net, rather as the beam trawler felt his trawl warp to check the

"Sausages". Five girdlines have been passed round the loaded sleeves and have been hove forward and secured on the rail in order to reach the cod end. Abaft the rigging a man with a mingle cuts off a cod, for his mates to slide it into the docking hose and sling it aboard.

bumping of the trawl over the ground. He knew if he had fish before he felt their weight, for as the sleeve filled it bulged and shortened, so that the first intimation on deck might be to find a few fathoms of slack pinion.

The usual practice was to "middle the water". For example, in nine fathoms the top baulk would be two fathoms below the surface and the lower baulk two fathoms off the ground. In very shallow water, however, the lower baulk rested on the bottom and the upper baulk was raised out of the water under the bowsprit by dispensing with the templines and hooking in the jib halyard on one side, and the foresail halyard, or baulk tackle, on the other side.

17

To get the net, the anchor chain was put on its dog and cleared off the windlass on to the port knighthead. The baulks were then closed by winching in the windchain. Then the forelint was reached either by a long boathook or by throwing a grapnel into it. The net was now hauled; with a light catch this could be done by hand, but if it was full girdlines were passed round it.

These were of two kinds. The chain girdline was a length of chain wolded with old canvas against chafe, with rope tails. Once the sleeve was girdled with this a thimble or jamming girdline could be passed round. This was a rope with a thimble spliced in one end. The other end was passed through the thimble and the girdline pulled tight like a snare. With a full sleeve the forward end would be secured by a thimble girdline and then several chain girdlines could be passed around at this point and worked aft. If the net bulged too much for a chain girdline to be got round it a thimble girdline could be hitched on to lengthen it.

The girdlines were now pulled forward by tackles, or sometimes by a rope rove through the baulk davit or through a block on the bowsprit traveller and taken back to the anchor windlass (necessitating both chains being put on dogs). The *Charlotte Ellen* had a sheave mounted on the fore end of her starboard rail.

When the cod end was reached the end section of fish was cut off, either by use of a mingle or by slipping a metal hoop on a staff over the end of the net. Tollesbury men used the mingle, Brightlingsea men the hoop. This cut off four or five bushels (a "cod") in the end of the sleeve, which was tied with a knot, made by passing a bight of net twice through a running noose in the pinion, and then passing the end of

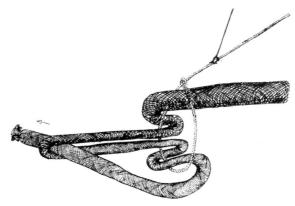

The cod end knot. A bight of net was passed twice through a running noose in the end of the pinion, and the docking hose and end of the last sleeve passed through the bight. The cod end bouy rope is seen rolling-hitched on the pinion. For clarity the net is shown distended; in practice it was limp, like an empty stocking.

the net through the bight. This knot was released and the first cod of fish slipped to the docking hose*, which was shaken to let the smig and fry go through the larger mesh before it was emptied through the hold scuttle hatch and the process repeated.

The mingle was a wooden tool having two handles, as on a scythe. At the bottom it had another length of wood at about forty-five degrees with a connecting link sometimes covered with a roller to save chafe on the net. The mingle was slipped down between the net and the smack's side, point aft, and turned through ninety degrees to cut off a cod.

*The docking hose was often referred to as the docanoes. This pleasant phonetic corruption generated its own singular — docanoe, as in "docanoe mesh" and "docanoe lacing". As a further complication it also came to be pronounced "dockarnose" with the accent on the second syllable. This example is a useful warning of the pitfalls and perils of etymology in this field!

The man with the mingle or hoop stood just abaft the rigging. The next man to him took the net off the mingle and together with the third man ran the fish down into the docking hose, the end of which was already held by the fourth man. The net was grabbed as the smack rolled to it, and "kneed" against the rail to hold it as she rolled back. "Navvy" Mussett sewed eight sennet strops on to his sleeve so that when the final cry of "Up and over!" came two men could grasp the strops that were uppermost and sling the "cod" into the hold better than by hooking their fingers into the meshes. This was done through the scuttle hatch, a small hatch abaft the main hatch, used not only in rough weather, when it could be dangerous to have a big hatch off the deck, but at all times because the smack trimmed better with the weight kept as far aft as possible.

Speed in shooting the gear was often essential with the fish coming down fast on the tide. "Navvy" Mussett claims that a trained crew could do the job in three minutes; Ken Francis considers that *Ellen's* crew could shoot faster than any other, but that five or six minutes would be the best time possible. It took about half an hour to get the net under normal conditions.

It was desirable to get the net when the tide was not running too hard (in heavy weather low water was ideal) to save labour for the crew and strain on the smack, but to avoid completely slack water, as a little tide kept the net afloat.

When the sleeves were full of fish they were, as has been mentioned, bulging and distended, and thus shorter than the total length of forty-five yards when empty. Even so, there was a problem to reach the pinion end where emptying had to start. This was overcome by pulling the net forward, and leaving loops between the girdlines hanging overboard like a string of giant sausages.

One way was to put, say, four girdlines round the net and heave the aft one forward. In this way three "sausages" were formed and could be secured. The "sausages" hung from their girdlines along the forward rail, and in releasing them it was important to let them go in the right order. The after-most "sausage" would come clear, but if another was let go in error there was a danger of it dropping through the jump hole. When this happened on a dark night, with the smack rolling and plunging, it was no joke.

During the First World War, when crews were short, Joe Francis had his son Jack, aged fifteen, and an older man who was by trade a chimney sweep as crew of the *Iris Mary*. Fishing in the Gilman Hole they had a full net when three large bights of fish secured on the bow by girdlines dropped down through the jump holes. With an inexperienced crew it took them thirty hours to clear the fouled net.

When fishing was complete the baulks were brought to the davit, and the baulk tackle, leading down the starboard rigging from the masthead, was hooked into a long link at the top of the chain. The baulks were hove up and came aft so that one end could be secured in a chock on deck and the other lashed outside the rigging. In this trim the smack sailed home.

The procedure described was used on "right-handed" smacks; that is, smacks with the anchor snatch to port and the bowsprit to starboard, the East Coast style. A few smacks were, however, "left-handed", that is with the anchor snatch and bowsprit reversed, the usual fashion down channel and on the west coast. Among these at Tollesbury were the *Laura* and

Arthur and Harry Death stowboating aboard the Ellen *of Rowhedge in the 1920s. They are passing girdlines round a sleeve, and have pulled a forward sleeve up on to main halyard to get it out of the way, having worked the fish aft from it.*

The left-handed smack Guide, *which came from Shoreham, with Albert Lewis's* Gladys.

The handspike windlass was the stowboater's only mechanical aid. It had to handle the anchor chain and cable, the windchain, the rope to haul the net forward, and the bobstay — no mean task. It was slow, but it was reliable and "it would lift hell and all".

the *Guide*, both of which came from Shoreham. These craft worked over the port side, with all the gear reversed; even to offsetting the jump holes to starboard.

There were also some variations with the introduction of motors, dealt with in chapter five, and the different procedures used by the Leigh bawleys are described in chapter six.

Swinging to the anchor at high or low water with the net set was dangerous because of the risk of the slack handfleets fouling the anchor. It could only be safely attempted where there was more than fifteen fathoms of water (the length of the handfleets), and the only place it was in fact regularly done was at the Tongue, off the North Foreland, where the biggest smacks lay for days on end. In shallower water, under favourable conditions, the smack was sometimes allowed to swing with the cable shortened up to bring the stringer up to the anchor snatch, but the usual procedure was to heave up the baulks close under the davit and shorten in on the anchor till the handfleets could be pulled in over the baulks and flaked out along the deck.

Another dreaded mix-up was the windmill, which occurred if the baulks cockbilled and crossed, perhaps through lying with the wind against the tide at slack water. This took a lot of clearing. "Navvy" Mussett once succeeded in recovering a windmill and running into the East Swale for refuge in a gale in which Ted Heard's *Edith* was lost on the Columbine. He lay there three weeks with the windmill frozen solid to

the deck. One of the favourite stowboating stories is of the skipper who turned in, overslept and found he had a slack water windmill. He rushed up on deck in his underpants and it was two days before he was able to put his trousers on.

In addition to the gear described, the stowboaters rigged a wire or wooden guard rail from the stem to the shrouds on each side to make the foredeck a less dangerous place, and aft they used washboards on each quarter to keep the gear on deck and some of the water off it. These had iron spigots which socketed into the thole pin holes in the rail. The port quarterboard was longer than the starboard one, since the maximum protection was needed on the port side for working, while the baulks would have fouled a longer quarterboard to starboard. These fittings were also used for stowing the handfleets and hip ropes — the forward lot on the guard rails, the after lot on a becket inside the washboards.

At the end of the season, in addition to getting the net, baulks, cable and other gear ashore, it will thus be seen that the baulk davit and tackle had to be unrigged, the stowboat anchor replaced by the lighter summer anchor, the quarterboards and bow rails and light boards unshipped, and the winter chocker pole replaced by the summer topmast, which, after the coming of motors, was usually left ashore for the sprat season.

CHAPTER THREE

The Luck of the Tides

THE STOWBOATERS were four-handed, working two watches of two men each, or occasionally they shipped six hands, which was ideal till it came to the shareout.

Payment was always by the share. The system with four hands was to have six shares, one for the boat, one for the net, one for each man. When a motor was introduced it took another half share, with the oil paid for out of the gross takings before the split. The hope was to make £100 a share by Christmas.

Before the days of echo sounders there was no guide but the gulls, which worked voraciously on sprat shoals, or "skoles" as they were usually called. Gulls working close to the water meant that fish were swimming near the surface, but when they were wheeling high it meant that the fish were deep.

The gulls then were very different in numbers, species and habits from those of today. Millions of blackheads, known as "spratbirds", sat on the water all over the estuary, and when cutting in their catches the smacks were obscured by them. It was easy to judge which smack had the best catch by the way the gulls divided their attentions. They were so tight-packed overhead that working on deck it was actually possible to pick them out of the air by hand, as their numbers made it impossible for them to get out of the way. The herring gull, now common, was not then seen. The changes are probably due not only to the end of spratting but also to the different methods of waste disposal ashore. Municipal rubbish was then incinerated; today

it is dumped in old sand workings, attracting the gulls ashore.

The chief fear was, of course, to catch no fish; the next was to catch too many. The very first time "Navvy" Mussett went stowboating they had sailed about for a week without seeing a gull working.

Then at the Horns (the Maplin Spit) they saw the *Volante* put to, and rounded up with her. The shoal struck them so solid that within half an hour the net was torn from the ropes, and they had twelve and a half tons of fish tangled in a quarter of a ton of net, all in a strong tide in thirteen fathoms of water. It took them thirteen hours' hard toil to clear that lot, but they had the consolation of a top price of 18s a bushel.

On another occasion "Navvy" tried a stand by the Barrow Sand, about half an hour before high water. The gulls came towards them in a white wall "like Dover Cliffs". They got twenty-five cod, and dabbed the net in again with the tide so slack they had to row the pinion out with the boat. As soon as it was out they got another good haul. Freddy Good of Harwich in the *Corsair* was nearby. He had little experience, and his gear came up on his port side. Instead of stropping his baulks together and dropping them down to sheer the smack across them he took the net round the stern to get it on the starboard side, a position which might have put him in a hopeless predicament with that weight of fish about, but with beginner's luck he got away with it.

Sometimes shoals were found without any

The atmosphere of Brightlingsea Creek in the short busy winter days is wonderfully captured in this study.

help from the gulls, indicated by one or two cormorants or diving birds. Joe Francis had such a knowledge of the run of the channels and the set of the tides that he knew where to expect sprats with an uncanny skill that looked like instinct but was, in fact, the result of careful observation and a profound store of experience. The tides in most places set northerly on the floods and southerly on the ebbs, and whether they were "making" or "taking off" also made a difference. Many a time the *Ellen* would up anchor and shift half a mile to the north for the flood tide or to the south for the ebb, with due allowance as to whether the tides were springs or neaps. An extra fathom of water could also make all the difference, specially when the

Brightlingsea Creek in the heyday. Skiffs loaded with barrels ply to the causeway from loaded smacks. In foreground is a heap of sprats, probably in a skiff lying ashore. A photo taken in 1936.

sprats were close in under the sands, and Joe Francis would keep his crew sounding for an hour till he found the extra three feet he was looking for. He did not consult a chart, seeming to have all the soundings in his head. A good compass and a leadline gave him all the help he asked.

Often there have been fifteen or twenty boats all stowboating within an area of a square mile and one vessel has caught 200 or 300 bushels where the remainder have a bushel or two of rubbish. One nice quiet day the *Ellen* had worked the flood tide under the Buxey with a catch of about two bushels and tried again the next day with no fish. After much discussion they decided to up anchor and cross over to the Whitaker, where they arrived at the South Buxey buoy just as the *Wonder* was heaving up her anchor. She had been there two days and had had no luck.

They anchored in almost the same place in the best of the water. It was high water at five, and as soon as it was possible they sunk away the gear and went below for tea. At eight o'clock they pulled the pinion and decided to heave up, finding about thirty cod of lovely fish. They then waited for the next flood and hove up again at three am, working in another forty cod. When the *Wonder* came out the next day the crew would not believe they had come from the very spot they had left.

The thinking behind that success was this; they had had a few fish earlier in the week under the Buxey but these had fallen off for a couple of days with the tides "making". This suggested that the shoal had gone up the Raysand Channel and perhaps into the Shore Ends. By crossing over to the Whitaker with the start of the neap tides they caught the fish coming down again. It was just bad luck that the *Wonder* did not stop for another two tides.

The strain on the smacks, let alone the smacksmen, was immense. The *Olive Branch* was lying off the North East Gunfleet when the wind came in easterly and she jumped so much that the skipper, Rickwood, was thrown over the bows by the windlass. Being strong, even for a stowboater, he came aboard again over the stern. They could not wait for slack water and in heaving up the smack burst her bow open, though she was able to limp home.

Riding in the Gilman Hole, near the Girdler, "Navvy" Mussett's *Bluebell* broke the foredeck beams due to the weight on the windlass and had to replace them with an iron girder. Replacements for windlass ironwork were supplied by Stanford's, the Colchester ironfounders, and at Southend Bundock's always kept a stock of pawl plates for their bawleys to save losing a day's fishing for repairs.

The *Paragon*, with "Navvy" Mussett aboard, and Joe Francis's *Olive* had run through the Spitway and were turning up the Wallet, triple reefed and heavy loaded, when they had to anchor. The *Paragon* opened her seams so that they had to get the planks fixed at Bradwell with three-inch screws before sailing to Brightlingsea to discharge. The *Olive*, a former Boston smack skippered by Bill Godfrey, was unluckier still, getting in irons a mile below the Knoll buoy. The anchor was let go and when she snubbed to forty-five fathoms of chain she buried her head in the sea and before they could stow the mainsail she started to sink. Probably the load of sprats broke down the fore bulkhead and ran into the foc's'le. The crew got into the row boat and grabbed the pinion, lying to it all night and baling the boat out till daylight when they were

Out of the hold and into the barrels. The sleeve of the smack in the foreground lies across the jump hole in the forelint of the smack behind.

The horses and carts could enter the water so that skiffs could unload direct on to them.

picked up by the sailing barge *Vera* and landed on Clacton Pier. The loss of the *Olive* was a bad blow to Joe Francis. She was a well-found vessel and that year a lot of money had been spent on her hull and gear and a completely new net. There was no reason for her to have foundered and as with all the smacks at that time there was no such thing as insurance.

The rivalry between the Brightlingsea and Tollesbury fleets was intense. "Navvy" Mussett always claimed that the Tollesbury men were the most enterprising stowboaters. This may have been to some extent pride in his adopted village, but as he was himself top boat three years running he had a right to his opinion. "Brightlingsea men were all right in the Wallet," he recalls. "But they didn't fancy getting up Swin."

The Brightlingsea men were equally convinced that they knew the tides and soundings in the Wallet far better than the Tollesbury men and could outfish them in home waters. The Tollesbury men were so often up Swin, they say, partly because they did not like to be beaten and partly because of the differences in the two ports. When the Brightlingsea men had discharged they could be home in a few minutes, whereas Tollesbury men had to sail out of the Colne into the Blackwater and up the creek to "The Leavings" where their smacks lay. They then had a long row to the Hard, or an equally long walk if they landed on the seawall. Consequently, they lived aboard in the Colne or in Brightlingsea Creek, and since they could not get home they might just as well be away in the Medway or under "Hungry Hill" in the Swale.

Certainly once one was the wrong side of the Spitway, that difficult and dangerous front door to home waters, the risk of being caught out in

the short, treacherous winter days increased. One year "Navvy" and Ted Heard were both bound home for Christmas in a hard northerly wind. Ted made it, and "Navvy" in the *Paragon* would have done so, but as the sea washed across her foredeck it carried the anchor chain through the bulwark and overboard. The Essex smacks, like the barges, always stowed the chain on deck with little or no provision to secure it, chiefly because a barrel windlass traverses the foredeck and allows no place for a hawsehole to feed the chain into a locker.

With twenty-five fathoms of chain hanging in the water the *Paragon* would not wend or go to windward, and the only thing they could do was to ruck down the peak and run back to the Medway. "It looks like blowing for a week," "Navvy" commented gloomily, and it did. They sailed across to Southend and put two young newly-married men ashore on the pier so they could get home; the others had their Christmas in Queenborough, under the lee of the glue factory, the stink of which would turn the strongest stomach. They attempted to sell the sprats for glue but were told that the factory had already tried them and gummed up their machines in doing to.

The chief consolation when lying wind-bound in Queenborough was the kind heart of the landlady of the Old House at Home. When the fishermen went up there for a wash she would lend soap and towels and when they were hard up she would even advance a pound.

Nor were wind and weather the only enemies. The Swin and the Barrow Deep are main shipping channels to and from the Port of London, and when the stowboaters put to there they were always in danger of being run down. Many hours have been spent ringing bells in fog and burning flares at night, and there have been numerous near-misses.

In December, 1932, the *Ellen*, skippered by Joe Francis, and the *Marion*, skippered by W Bishop, were anchored with their gear down two cables north of the North Knob buoy at night. Aboard *Ellen* all hands were on deck watching the shipping passing to the nor'ard when suddenly a tanker of some 8,000 tons sheered towards them. They burned flares and it was some time before she altered course, coming so close that they got into the row boat ready to shove off. She missed the *Ellen* but did not quite clear the *Marion*, whose bowsprit ran along the tanker's quarter till suddenly her bow was pulled almost under water. Then she broke adrift. The tanker's propeller had cut through her chain and she started to drift with her gear under her. The *Ellen*'s crew boarded their gear and went to the assistance of the *Marion*, whose crew were badly shaken up. It took two hours to retrieve her gear, after which they escorted her to Brightlingsea. The tanker did not stop, but eventually her name was discovered and *Marion*'s owner received compensation. *Ellen*'s crew got five pounds each.

One foggy day a mile below the Whitaker Spit a small coaster collided with the *Ellen*, knocking down several timber heads, bulwarks and quarterboards on the starboard side. This coaster also did not stop and though they boarded their gear they were not fast enough to catch her as she steamed through the Spitway and down the Wallet. Next day Ken Francis and his father travelled to Ipswich Dock and there was the coaster with the *Ellen*'s green and stone colour paint all along her starboard side. After several weeks they received compensation for the damage and loss of time.

An almost identical experience befell the *Express* thirty years before this. Soon after Christmas, 1898, she was working in the Edinburgh, the tide flooding and approaching high water. About four am the mate on watch saw a large steamer coming up the channel and shaping to pass to the north of the smack. When only a short distance away she put her helm to starboard and started to come across the bows of the *Express*. Seeing that a collision was inevitable, the mate roused out the other five hands and all bar one were in the boat by the time the steamer caught the smack's chain, carrying away her bowsprit and pulling her stern nearly out of the water and her bow under till the water was up to the foc's'le hatch. The sixth man would not risk the deck for fear of the mast falling, but it held, though bowed over her head. Suddenly the chain broke and the *Express* was adrift, but still in one piece.

The steamer went on her way without even slowing down, and the *Express* was sailed up to Billingsgate where the skipper, Captain Abram Norton, sent a telegram to the owner, Mr Went. He and the Brightlingsea Lloyd's agent, Mr A A Jefferies, who was also secretary of the smacks' insurance club, immediately set off for London, where on examining the damage they were astonished that the smack could have survived.

The next task was to trace the steamer. Unfortunately, none of the men could give much information as to the number of masts or funnels, or anything to identify her. All they knew was that her bottom was painted red, for the end of the broken cable was this colour. At last someone suggested that as the ship scraped along the smack's side something might have been broken off her. They searched the tangle of damaged gear on deck and in it found a piece of

The coming and going of the skiffs. Below is the Masonic, *with Harry Death, who was also skipper of Miss Carstairs' yacht* Sonia.

The narrow escape of the Express. *Based on a drawing in the* Wide World Magazine, *February, 1908.*

metal which did not belong. On being straightened out it proved to be the fly end of a small arrow, painted buff, one end bright from a recent fracture. A man went aloft to examine the outer end of the starboard crosstree and found this was marked by the same buff paint.

It was not much to go on. Inquiry at the Custom House revealed that the accident had not been reported, but provided a list of the previous day's arrivals. The three men, skipper, owner and Lloyd's agent, set out to examine them. After a long and weary tour of inspection the old skipper suddenly pointed to the boat hanging in the quarter davits of one of the last on the list. The boat had a piece nicked out of the ornamental badge on her bow, and they judged that the height was the same as the smack's crosstree. Going aboard, they found their piece fitted perfectly, and demanded to meet the owners.

The tale so far was written up by Mr Jefferies and published in the *Wide World Magazine* (February, 1908) under the title "The Broken Arrow; A Marine Detective Story". He refrained from including the account of the subsequent interview with the owners which, however, remains in his unpublished memories. The same three men presented themselves before the manager of the biggest shipping company in the world in his splendid office. After keeping them standing in front of him for some time while he finished his correspondence, he abruptly enquired, "Well, what do you want?" The skipper and owner were too tongue-tied to answer, but Jefferies, according to himself, replied, "Your ship yesterday morning in coming up the Edinburgh collided with the smack *Express* and did very considerable damage and as your ship was entirely to blame we want you to pay for it.

" 'Ho!' he said. 'You have no right to fish in the way of navigation and I don't admit liability.'

"I replied with due respect, 'Sir, we have as much right to fish in the open water as you have to navigate your ship there, provided we comply with the laws which regulate navigation and fishery, which we had done on the smack and which you did not do on your ship.' And I added that I had been many times in the Admiralty courts in the city. The old boy settled down better after this and arranged matters of survey, etc, and finally settled the matter in an amicable way without recourse to law."

As well as the clumsiness of steamboats the stowboaters had to worry about the boorishness of the London muck boats, whose skippers' manners were sometimes as coarse as their cargoes.

In the Black Deep, their dumping ground, the "Bovril boats", as they were sarcastically named, would open their bottoms and release a hundred tons of filth just above an anchored smack instead of troubling to get downtide of her. Closing the baulks was not enough; the fishermen would have to jettison their catch and clean out the filthy objects thrummed in their nets before they could start again.

CHAPTER FOUR

The Gamble of the Market

EVEN WHEN the smack had let go her anchor in Brightlingsea Creek there was still plenty to do.

The fish oil had to be washed from the great nets, which then had to be dried. For this the forelint was pulled up on the baulk tackle or a halyard and the net was led under the boom. Then, with the sail stowed on its gaff and pulled up clear, the net was flaked in bights over the boom, with a bight of sleeve at the masthead on a halyard.

Next the buyers had to be dealt with. They were concerned with the freshness and the quality of the catch. There was nothing you could do about freshness bar hard lying. One buyer was always known as "Sniffy" because he began sampling the catch with his nose long before he had reached the smack and could inspect it with his eyes. Even if the smack had been fishing for a week the assurance was always the same: "All yesterday's fish."

Quality depended on the luck of the shoal, but you could make the best of what you had. The buyers knew that the biggest fish ran down to the sides as the docking hose was shot through the scuttle hatch. "I want five bushels out of the wings", they would demand. With fish in baskets the best could be brought to the top by vigorous bucketing down, which improved the look of the sample. This procedure was known as "sugaring".

Bill White, buyer for Tabor's, always jumped down the hold and drew his sea boot through the fish to test the quality by the amount of "sniff" clinging to his boots. Sometimes he would shoot a bucketful of sprats on deck and cull the large, medium and small in different heaps to sample the quality. This, the answer to the fishermen's "sugaring", was known as "shading".

It was generally accepted by the buyers, and by the pickling and canning firms, that Wallet sprats were larger and better than those caught in the Swin and other channels. Joe Francis always maintained that the first of the Wallet fish generally came up along the Suffolk shore and were those missed by the drift netters of Kessingland, Aldeburgh and Southwold. Another theory he had was that if the shoals came into the estuary from seaward and settled in the Swin or Barrow Deeps the larger mature fish separated out and worked to the nor'ard into the Wallet. Wallet fish sometimes realised up to a shilling a bushel extra. The Middle Deep by contrast produced the smallest fish, in fact if the buyers knew a smack had been fishing there they would not go near her. Sprats caught in the Whitaker had blue backs, instead of the usual green tinge.

The nature of the sprat market in old days is largely guesswork. Sometimes smacks sailed to Billingsgate or to Chatham to unload; sometimes if they were up Swin they would sell a sleeve of fish to a Leighman who would tow it to his bawley or peter boat and sail away with it to London. Probably a lot of boats sold what they could on Hythe Quay, Colchester, hawked some round the town and let the rest go for manure.

Barrels, carts and skiffs keep the Hard busy. Below: Washing in readiness for pickling.

By the heyday, however, Brightlingsea was established as the spratting centre. Several firms were pickling up to 8,000 bushels a day, in brine with spices and bay leaves, and two or three ships a year came into the river to load a thousand barrels for Poland, Germany, Russia or Scandinavia. The pickling ingredients were bay leaves, Spanish hops, cloves, sandalwood, pimento, sugar and salt, dissolved in brine. Sprats were also barrelled and iced and sent by the Harwich train ferry to Ostend, as many as 2,000 bushels on some occasions, in barrels holding three and a half bushels.

Consignments of fresh fish were sent almost daily to the London market and to the Midlands. This trade was carried on chiefly by the oyster merchants, Tabor, Musson, Day, White, Eagle and Minter, who dispatched anything between ten and forty bushels at a time, using mainly grape barrels which took two bushels.

Despite the development of the Brightlingsea market in the 1930s, some smacks still sailed to Billingsgate in living memory. Jack Francis recalls taking 408 bushels there and selling them

for £18. During the unloading the buyer went bad on his bargain but after a row took half for £12 10s. In disgust Jack sailed for home on a Monday night, arriving on Thursday to find no fish at Brightlingsea and the buyers hungry. One of them took a fancy to the remaining half cargo and offered to buy them and send them to Billingsgate. "The buggers have been there once already", observed Jack. But the buyer dipped each basket in the water to freshen the fish up a bit before tipping them into grape barrels, and afterwards declared it was one of the best deals he ever did.

Sprats were also smoked, principally by Musson's in their premises at the bottom of Tower Street, but some fishermen also had smoke houses, which were usually about two feet six inches square and seven feet high. The best and biggest sprats were washed in fresh water to remove their scales, then laid in salt for seven or eight hours, then washed again in fresh water and hung on metal spits in the smoke house over a fire of oak chips damped down with oak sawdust, obtained from the shipyards.

The smoke house had a vent in the top to give a good circulation of smoke, and seven or eight hours' smoking was needed to give them a fine golden colour. Before Christmas they were so full of oil that a longer time was needed.

The surplus for manure was loaded into railway trucks at Wivenhoe, into tumbrils at St Osyth mill quay or into lighters or skiffs in Brightlingsea Creek. The smacksmen used to caulk the sides of the railway trucks with mud to keep the water in, and as the truck went on the weighbridge at Wivenhoe they would run round to the blind side and swing from it to add to the weight.

These surplus fish fetched about 4½d a bushel and the average price of pickling on the fresh market was from 9d to half-a-crown. Ken Francis recalls his best trip was in the *Ellen* in 1931 when they got 6s 6d for 302 bushels — just over £98. The all-time record week's work was claimed by the Brightlingsea *Masonic* with 3,000 bushels, and the top price was £1 a bushel in 1914.

As well as the pickling yards there were also some canneries. Soon after the First World War James Edgar and Son of Deal opened up a works at the Hythe, Colchester. The catches were mostly unloaded and sorted at Wivenhoe and only the larger fish were sent on up the river for canning. Edgar's also had the ex-German schooner *Gloria* (remembered for her spectacular destruction by fire at Heybridge, near Maldon, in the late 1930s) lying in the Colne, fitted with a fishmeal plant so that the smacks could go alongside and get rid of fish they could not sell ashore.

By the 1930s Edgar's cannery was in liquidation and the Brightlingsea pickling yards in decline, but at Wivenhoe North Sea Canners Ltd was established in 1932 by Mr Lewis Worsp, who bought some of Edgar's machinery and converted part of the former Wivenhoe shipyard into a factory which produced a million tins a year, mostly under North Sea Brisling labels. With average fish, a bushel filled a hundred cans. About a quarter went to the Navy where they were specially popular in the seamen's messes and they were also exported worldwide. The firm succeeded in selling a hundred cans for just over £1 in Australia and continued till the sprat fishery finally folded about 1960. At first North Sea Canners bought on the market but later, in the Larsen trawling era, it owned its own smacks, including the specially built *Essex Girl* and *Fisher Girl*, and had a full-time contract with others.

Soon after the Second World War British Fish Canners also thought enough of the trade at its Leeds factory to open up a small cannery at the Hythe, Colchester, which contributed to the market for two or three years.

Three sailing barges in Fieldgate's Dock, Brightlingsea. They were lightering to a steamer lying in the Colne, bringing in empty barrels, seen being rolled ashore down a ladder, and taking off full barrels, seen in background, for Sweden.

Stowboater putting out sprats at St Osyth. The maltings shown were burned down in 1920, and the photo probably dates from well before the first world war, for both barges are tiller-steered and that on left has her undressed mizzen mounted on the rudder head. She has an extraordinary mixed cargo (or "cotchel freight") with a huge stack on the foredeck, and barrels, probably from Parry's oil mill at Colchester, on her main hatch.

Once "Navvy" came into Brightlingsea in the *Bluebell* with a fine catch of first class sprats. Going ashore to the Anchor he took a bucketful with him, as was his custom, for Elsie was always obliging there with an "icebreaker" at any hour of the morning. Served in the kitchen, this consisted of a pint of hot Bovril and a double rum. He was fishing that year for the Leeds factory, represented by Joe Ruffle, and getting 4s a bushel, but in the Anchor he met Ken Francis's uncle, George, who was buying for Worsp's North Sea Canners at Wivenhoe. The two were keen summer rivals in twelve-metres, for George was Sir William Burton's skipper and "Navvy" was skipper of "Fiddler" Payne's *Vanity V.*

"Beautiful sample," said George. "Pity you're fishing for Ruffle." "I'm fishing for myself," said "Navvy". "I've got 400 bushels all like that, fresh out. You better 6s a bushel and the last shilling is yours."

In the morning George Francis was aboard and bid 6s. Joe Ruffle came soon after and bid 7s 6d. Francis went to 10s. "Those bloody fish were sold last night in the Anchor," observed Ruffle in disgust. "You're right," said "Navvy". "And it's a pity you didn't think to offer me a proper price before." "I hadn't got the money with me," "Navvy" recalls, "but as soon as I got home I wrote him a cheque for 484s. So his share was better than mine."

But they weren't all £200 catches by any means. Too often long, bitter nights with the deck awash and everything a dangerous struggle meant a glutted market and a few pence a bushel for muck. Great heaps of sprats lay on the Hard at Brightlingsea and Wivenhoe with buckets of filthy water thrown over them to deter pilferers, waiting for the farm carts to come and spread them on the fields.

Payments to buyers, which "Navvy" Mussett admits he had to make at a rate of 10s a hundred bushels, were acceptable as a commission on a bonanza, but they degenerated into corruption.

Things came to a head when Ben Heard in the *Volante*, Bobby Leavett in the *Bertha,* and "Navvy" Mussett in the *Bluebell* came in with 200 bushels of fine fish. The rule was first in first cleared, and "Navvy" hailed the buyer to tell him the order. He got no more than a grunt in reply, and when the other smacks came in full he went to them instead. The 200 bushels had to be dumped, but "Navvy" got on the phone to the Leeds factory and after spending 15s on three calls told the manager, Mr Banks, to look at the rubbish he would be receiving. Mr Banks was as good as his word. He was down at Brightlingsea within a day or two and fired the buyer.

Out of this incident came the foundation in the early 1950's of Tolfish Ltd, one of the very few attempts at a co-operative to be tried by the independent-minded Essex fishermen. As well as hiring its own landing quay it established an office at Brightlingsea, basing communication on the radio from the now defunct *Bluebell* and preserving the charade that she was still afloat to avoid obtaining a Post Office licence for ship-to-shore communication. By using an old landing craft and a few skiffs from Brightlingsea, Tollesbury was for the first time established as a landing port.

Herrings were occasionally caught. The Blackwater shoals, which since the end of the spratting have been the inshore fishermen's staple, were then neglected because the North Sea herring filled the market. But in the 1930's Tabor's installed marinating machines to deal with herrings. Basil Steady, who had the *Sunbeam* and later the *Alberta*, liked to stand off Bradwell and go ashore in his boat to set snares over the wall. He had to be back by slack water and reckoned that a hundred bushels of herring and three or four rabbits represented a reasonable tide's work.

The *Ellen* also made a few trips for 100 to 120 bushels and actually made one haul to order. Early in April, 1936, at 7.30 am they were debating whether to go to sea or not when Tabor's buyer, Bert Durrant, bet Jack Francis, then skipper of the *Ellen* and later foreman of the Colchester Oyster Fishery, two pints of beer that he and his brother Ken could not catch 300 bushels of herrings and be back in the creek by dinner time. They steamed to the North West Knoll, put their gear in and within half an hour the net surfaced full. They got under weigh with 350 bushels in the hold and anchored in Brightlingsea Creek at ten past one.

Once in the *Odd Times* "Navvy" made a freak haul of pilchards. They jammed the sleeves, which floated on the surface "like a Zeppelin", and filled every mesh right to the forelint, which they had to cut to get the gear at all. They spent two hours baling out fish and sailed for Wivenhoe loaded with twelve tons.

There Mr Worsp had no tins big enough to can them, but he got on to Shippam's, who luckily had two lorries in the area. They were paid for 11½ tons and gave half a ton away as well as taking six bags home. The fish gilled in the forelint were broken-backed, so they threw them away to the gulls, which when the tide went lay on the mud so gorged they could not move.

CHAPTER FIVE

The Old Order Passes

SOME MEN hated stowboating and dreaded the season; others enjoyed it and looked forward to it. Mankind is divided into those who love to go a-roving and those who prefer to sleep in their own beds every night. "Navvy" Mussett and Ken Francis both revelled in it. "All the time I was stowboating I was as happy as all the birds in the air," Ken recalls. And many of the younger generation who were just old enough to take part in the last few seasons feel they were privileged to have known an older, Homeric way of life, now quite passed away. Perhaps despite the miniscule nature of the quarry stowboating, with its free-ranging style, had more of the essence of hunting in it than most other forms of fishing. Certainly it offered the excitement of a gamble, absent from the steady toil of shrimping and oyster dredging.

It was a remarkably smelly trade, for the oil which ran from sprats had a pungent quality all its own. This "sprat gravy", as it was called, soaked the smacks' timbers and impregnated the smacksmen's clothing. If you went aboard a stowboater for ten minutes and then sat down in front of the fire at home anyone else in the room would soon know where you had been. "Navvy" Mussett recalls being in a pub with his mate one night when a toff came in. "Funny smell in here tonight," he observed to the landlord. Presently he inquired of "Navvy", "Do you fellahs work on the sewahs?" Assuring him to the contrary "Navvy" sidled up closer to him, whereupon he drank up his gin and tonic and departed. Once when the fleet was windbound in Queen-

Alberta *under power. The baulks are in their stowed position with net stowed on them probably for washing. The handfleets lie over the bow rail and a block is fixed below the bowsprit traveller for hauling net forward. The baulk tackle is hooked in the foredeck guard rail. Having a motor, she has no gaff or peak halyard, but merely a triangular "leg of mutton" mainsail.*

borough the men decided to go to the pictures. As they made themselves comfortable in the warm cinema they were surprised to see all the other members of the audience getting up and retreating to the furthest seats.

Stowboating also meant cold, hardship and disappointment. In fine weather it could be a pleasant occupation, with one man on deck watching the pinion and the rest below, with the stove glowing and on it the tea kettle, around which life below revolved. Teapots were not used; the kettle was always on the fire and tea was spooned in till it would no longer hold four cups of water. If the smack missed a day or two through bad weather the same brew went on the fire as soon as it was lit again. Dick Harman recalls how he sometimes lifted the lid with the poker to catch it before it overboiled, just as a sea hit the hot stovepipe. Not all the flying soot and scale missed the open kettle, so it was a rough brew. Yet the first time he had to empty it he found to his surprise a black oblong object at the bottom, and asked Dennis Heard what it was. He explained that it was a bit of wood and for God's sake not to chuck it away as it stopped the tea tasting smokey.

Such tea parties were very snug and sociable, at any rate if you like your tea that way, but in the days of sail it was no joke to stand to on a calm day and then have to get ten tons of sprats aboard in an easterly gale in the dark, with the prospect of pulling down a pair of reefs for a long, hard thrash home, decks in the water, with a glutted market at the end of it all.

The smacks went away for a week or a fortnight and one year "Navvy" Mussett only got home three times before Christmas. The rewards sound pitiful by present standards, but these were the days when a farm labourer

The motor joined in ashore as well as afloat in the 1930s. But Norfolk's lorry could not get its feet wet by unloading straight out of the skiffs, as the carts did.

earned thirty shillings a week and to make £4 in a factory meant a long week of unrelieved toil. The stowboater was his own master and he was always cheered on by the prospect of making a month's money in a tide. Since most of the smacksmen were yacht hands, on a winter retainer of £1 a week, there was the extra satisfaction that the share came as a bonus. Certainly the fishermen were usually able to build their own houses before the shipyard workers could — as good an index as any of economic prosperity then.

The best days were after the introduction of motors. Most of the Tollesbury boats fitted 13-15hp Kelvins between 1922 and 1924, in which year the first Brightlingsea boats followed suit, mostly with 9hp Thorneycroft petrol-paraffin engines. These were *Ellen*, *Claude*, *Boy Kenneth* and *Wonder*. With the introduction of engines the after cabins were given up (as in the case of sailing barges) and the sail lockers forward were converted into cabins — the position always used in the little class three oyster smacks.

With the first diminutive engines, the smacks would not motor as fast as they sailed, but the little auxiliaries took some of the weight off the job. The heavy, elaborate and costly cable was dispensed with, for the motor would ease the strain on the chain as well as on the smacksman toiling at his windlass bars. Using chain the smacksman would sometimes winch in twenty-five fathoms with a sprat "thrummed" in almost every link.

With a motor it was also possible, having shot the gear, to sheer the smack about in the tide into the path of an approaching shoal instead of having to see it pass by a smack's length away. Or, if the skipper fancied a short shift for the next tide, he could board his baulks aforehead and steam to his new position. This meant stropping the baulks snug under the davit with the net pulled up on the main halyards and the handfleets fleeted along the deck so that the stringer could be unshackled and the anchor hove just clear of the ground.

Possibilities hitherto undreamed of were also opened up by a motor. When sprats were in the Colne the *Ellen* took advantage and made three shoots in one day. The first, by the creek buoy on the last of the flood, produced 120 bushels; then it was out again on the ebb for another 200 by the Inner Bench Head and finally she got a further 250 bushels on the next flood by the North Eagle.

On another occasion the fleet were all gathered to the south'ard of the Knoll. It was high water about four pm when the fleet began to put to, and the *Ellen* decided to have a go just to the

nor'ard of the others. They pulled the pinion after about half an hour and found about twenty cod. Heaving up straight away they steamed down for about a mile and put to again. No sooner had they done so than they found they had another twenty cod. Once again they steamed down about another mile for yet another twenty cod. Being young and energetic, with lighter gear than the others, the Francis brothers had a reputation with the older men as madcaps, and as they passed "Diddy" Finch in the *Kingfisher* they heard the old chap grumble, "Don't seem no such thing as a quiet bloody time no more."

The early little motors were characters in their own right. Dick Harman was in the *Charlotte Ellen* which had hand starting. The *Betsan* boasted a six-volt electric starter, and they watched Roy Lewis press his button and disappear out of the creek before starting to crank their handle. After two hours Dennis Heard threw down the handle in disgust. "No wonder we can't get a living," he observed bitterly. "You two must be about 1½ volts each, 'cos I know I'm as strong as a torch battery."

Malcolm MacGregor went as a teenage boy with Dennis Heard and Dick Harman in the *Charlotte Ellen*. They were motoring up Swin over the ebb and he was alone on deck with the other two turned in below. After a while he heard Dennis shout up through the hatch, "You're too far to the south'ard. Look out or you'll be ashore." There was no way of looking out from a smack's cabin, so the skipper must have been able to tell from the sound of the propeller that they were in shallow water, and known that with the ebb tide they would be to the south'ard — evidence that new seamanly

arts developed as partial replacement for those which passed away with sail.

Later on the same voyage they ran into bitter weather with freezing fog, and again Malcolm was alone on deck, this time ringing the bell. He had had no sleep longer than a two-hour spell for three days, and at three am he came down below for a few minutes to get warm. The

The modern method. The Larsen trawler's cod end, in its strong reinforcing net, is slung aboard by a winch — a far cry from the stowboater's mingle and hoop.

moment he sat down he fell fast asleep and slumped over the hot stove. Dick Harman sprang up to save him but the old skipper never moved. "Just look at that boy," he observed. "Don't take the slightest interest in his work. I doubt we shan't never make a fisherman of him."

All this parallels the golden age of the East Coast trawling and herring drifting, which by common consent was introduced by the first steam drifters. But in both cases the engine which at first lightened the labour was not long in ruining the trade. For as power increased it was no longer necessary to fish for sprats at anchor or for herrings with drift nets, while the trawlermen were able to tow ever heavier and more destructive otter gear. Mid-water trawls could also now be used, usually between pairs of powerful motor smacks. Instead of being held stationary in the tide between baulks the net could now be driven through the water, extended by paravane kites developed in war time for mine sweeping.

Larsen trawling, as it was named after its Scandinavian inventor, was at first more productive and profitable than stowboating. It was, in "Navvy" Mussett's view, never so enjoyable, for although the trips could be shorter (few inshore fishermen now turn in aboard) he was on his feet from going aboard to coming ashore, watching over the echo sounder, manoeuvring to keep station with his "pair" boat and within a few years worrying over his radio and his Decca navigator.

Occasionally during the twenty-five years since mid-water trawling replaced stowboating the traditional harvests have been taken. The last at Tollesbury was in February, 1959, when at the very end of a blank season, described as the worst for twenty-five years, four smacks had hauls of up to 300 bushels. Two others had gone to Boston to fish in the Wash and four were laid up. Tolfish Ltd was still in existence but not active.

Since then the Essex trade has dwindled almost out of existence. The demand for fresh sprats has gone, smoking is now too laborious and the pickling yards and canneries have long since closed. As a result, when occasionally shoals succeed in returning to their old haunts the catches are no longer carefully packed in barrels, but are unloaded by grab at Colchester Hythe Quay to go to the fishmeal factories for pet food. Before blaming this on to the new techniques one must remember the charges levied against the stowboats when they were introduced, but it seems beyond all real doubt that man's greed and ingenuity have finally outdone him.

For while the stowboat net cut a bold slice out of a shoal unlucky enough to strike it, the mid-water pair trawlers, each running a diesel of 100hp instead of the modest nine hp with which the smacks were first satisfied, could follow and harry, cutting through first from one direction and then from another till there was little left. The few survivors were then probably swept up by the lethal German, Polish and Russian factory ships which have scavenged the North Sea, exterminating the thousand-year-old herring shoals.

It is a pity, for the stowboat net died just when there were wonderful opportunities to improve it. "Navvy" Mussett would dearly love to make a net today out of synthetic twine and rope. There was little to recommend the four-inch bass hip ropes, the stiff tarred splices, the rotting twine lints and sleeves, when one considers the equivalent available today, which would make a net half as heavy, bulky and tide-resistant, twice as strong and ten times as long-lasting.

There is need today for legal restrictions on inshore fishing, if offshore boats are not to destroy once productive seasons in a few short deadly raids. It would be a turn of fortune if after 500 years the once prohibited stall boat was finally approved as preferable to its more lethal successors.

Leigh bawley in light airs. She is shrimping, not stowboating.

CHAPTER SIX

The Whitebaiters

THE OTHER chief stronghold of the stowboat was further up the Thames Estuary, where the rivalry between Leigh and Southend was as keen as that between Brightlingsea and Tollesbury. Here there were two fisheries — for sprats and for whitebait. Whitebait, the mixed fry of fish of all species*, has always been prolific in the Thames Estuary, and has for centuries been esteemed as a delicacy in city restaurants, eaten with brown bread and butter, garnished with lemon and cayenne pepper, and washed down with iced punch.

Its annual day of glory was the Whitebait Feast, held till 1894 at Greenwich or Blackwall and traditionally attended by Cabinet Ministers and leading politicians. It marked the close of the Parliamentary session and was held on Trinity Monday (Whit Monday) or the nearest convenient day. It originated in Essex as a private dinner, annually enjoyed by some of the landed gentry who had been connected with the long and costly schemes to repair the great Thameside tidal inundation of 1707 known as the Dagenham Breach. The host, Sir Robert Preston, MP for Dover, invited distinguished guests either to the Breach House or to his "fishing cottage" nearby. The Prime Minister, William Pitt the Younger, became a regular diner up to the time of his death, but asked for a venue closer to London. To suit him Greenwich was chosen, and the local delicacy, whitebait, adopted.

The feast was revived in 1934 by Southend Chamber of Trade Commerce and Industry as part of a Whitebait Festival. This opens with the blessing of the catch, with ministers of five denominations taking part in a ceremony which was held at the end of the famous pier till it was burnt down in 1976. After the blessing a whitebait lunch was served in the town, attended by the Mayor, MPs and other local dignitaries, followed by a banquet in the evening to which well-known speakers were invited as well as the luncheon company. In 1974 it was recognised that two feasts in a day, even of whitebait, were taxing both appetites and

---

*The exact nature of whitebait has long aroused heated dispute. The naturalist Frank Buckland identified in it:— herrings, sprats, gobies, weavers, sand eels, smelts, pipe fish, sticklebacks, buntings (or brown shrimps), red shrimps, gorbils or garpike. Murie added to this list (including flatfish taken in drag nets), sand smelts, shad, eels, eel pouts, white gobies, plaice, dabs, flounders, soles, bass, mullet, lump fish, sea horse, lampries, crabs, isopods, opposum shrimps, octopus, star fish and jelly fish. Yet Holdsworth was still insisting in 1883 that whitebait "should be pretty well known now to be nothing but young herrings". As if the subject exasperated him, he added for good measure, "So difficult is it to get rid of popular delusions that we will venture to prophesy that at any time within the next fifty years, or perhaps longer, the question as to what the whitebait is will be brought up and discussed in the newspapers with as much as earnestness as if it were an entirely new problem and created in perfect ignorance of it having been shown that after the most searching examination no difference can be discovered between young herrings and the most orthodox whitebait."

This aggressive insistence probably derives from the same hostility on the part of the herring fishery which 500 years ago led to the prohibition of the stowboat. In fact, while small quantities of so many species are found in it whitebait does consist principally of the fry of herrings and of sprats, which are identical to the eye but may be distinguished by the fact that the underside of one is rough to the finger and of the other smooth.

purses. Moreover it was difficult to attract speakers at the end of September, the date when the blessing of the catch is always carried out, so the evening banquet was moved to November. In this form the Festival continues to the present day.

Until the nineteenth century whitebait was a fishery of Greenwich and Gravesend, and it was up-river pollution which drove it down to Leigh, with the railway and the pier at Southend making marketing practicable at the same time.

The Greenwich stow nets were miniatures, with mouths only three feet square. They were fixed to the sides of boats lying in the tideway, dipping not more than four feet below the surface. The hose was pulled in and emptied periodically. When fishing as far upstream as Woolwich it was necessary to wait for the tide to have flowed three or four hours and the water to be brackish to the taste before bait was found, in times when there must have been more fresh water coming down than there is today. Seine nets were also employed in Woolwich and Blackwall reaches.

As the fishing was driven downriver the Leigh bawleys were developing in size to make them capable of using full size gear, and it may be assumed that they copied the stow nets of the North Essex smacks, or "vessels" as they were respectfully called by the bawleymen, for the same twenty-one foot baulks and thirty foot gap were adopted, with generally similar gear and names, though the up-and-downs were called "fennels" and the forelint was termed "the wides". Around 1920, however, the Leigh and Gravesend bawleys began to find it convenient for fishing in shallow water to dispense with the short stringer and to attach the handfleets

"Whitebait fishing", from the Illustrated London News, *June 3, 1848. This drawing of Greenwich Reach, by Duncan, shows, according to the accompanying article: "The net with its wooden framework fixed to the side of the boat". In fact it does not. And the artist also shows the oars shipped and the anchor on the rail, although the text describes the boat as "moored in the tideway". Nevertheless, it gives an impression of the little peterboats, with a canvas-covered tilt for a cabin, used in the mid-19th century in the upper reaches of the estuary.*

directly to the anchor with a string chain fifteen fathoms long*.

The whitebaiters never adopted long sleeves, for their catches were smaller. Instead of the forty-five yards used by the Tollesbury and Brightlingsea men they were content with fourteen or fifteen feet of fine mesh net tarred to give it stiffness, and derisively called the "sweat rag". A whitebaiter would wear out two sweat rags a season. Young's, one of the merchants mentioned below, also employed whitebait

stowboaters in the Crouch, but the trade did not extend north of this.

Employment by merchants and companies was commoner than in north Essex; indeed, the trade was dominated by the merchants Beecroft, Bundock, Coverley, Bridge and Brazier, Kingsland, Myall, Wakeland, Young and Osborne. The biggest of these was William Young and Son, which moved down from Greenwich at the end of the nineteenth century, and was built up by William Joseph Young, the "whitebait king", who died in 1943. After diversifying into shrimps at Leigh and white fish at Grimsby the

*This is stated both by Dr Murie and by Edgar March: *Inshore Fishing Craft*, vol one, which also says that handfleets were called hemlets. Cecil Osborne, however, only knew the term handfleet, and always rigged them conventionally, shackled in the anchor chain, of which fifteen fathoms were used, with fifteen fathoms of rope cable.

Blessing the catch at a Southend whitebait festival.

Young Group of Companies has become one of the biggest concerns of its kind in the world, though its whitebait fishing has now been transferred to Perthshire. When his fishery was at its height at Leigh William Young was known to order five tons of fish to be delivered in his garden for manure.

Being under group management the Leigh boats often fished in fleets for baiting and shrimping, though not for fish trawling. From two to twenty boats would work together. According to Murie, every boat would down anchor and down sail and swing to the tide together, having, if possible, kept clear of each other. They went out provisioned for a week, and some would sail home on Saturday, returning on Monday with provisions for the others. This fleeting was extended to spratting, as described in the next chapter.

The whitebait trade was dominated by the need to get the fish to market fresh, a problem increased by the fact that all attempts to keep bait alive in well boats failed. For this reason there was no question of long voyages or mammoth catches. It was primarily an overnight and early morning trade, so that the catch could be put on a morning train to Fenchurch Street where special horse traps were awaiting to take it to Billingsgate. For this purpose, Southend, with its pier accessible at all states of tide and a better train service, was at first preferred to Leigh where, however, facilities were gradually improved. In 1898 Leigh had nine decked smacks and sixteen open lug sail or rowboats at work, with a steady increase going on. The rowboats were used for drag netting, introduced as the result of Thames Conservancy bylaws passed in 1893, limiting fishing above the conservancy boundary which lay between the Yantlet Beacon in Kent and the Crowstone on the Essex side.

The trade was also at this time extending its season. Traditionally, whitebait had been in season from the opening to the closing of Parliament, that is from February to August, but now the demand made it profitable all the year round, and it was found that drag nets served best in summer after May. These nets were forty fathoms long, and nine feet deep at the ends. In the middle, or bunt, the depth was fifteen feet, and here a pocket, fifteen feet long, was let in. According to Murie the sides of this pocket were panels of one inch smelt net, two fathoms deep, with a central part one-third to one-half inch mesh. This is not an entirely clear description, and probably the cod end rather than the central part was fine mesh.

The Kentish sprat drifters at Deal and Walmer also used drag seines where the beaches were clean enough, but in the days before synthetic material was available these small mesh nets rotted when idle and it was difficult to get enough use out of them to make them pay for themselves.

The Leigh whitebait stowboaters had a crew of two, working three shares, the third being for the boat. For drag netting an extra hand was engaged for 12s to 15s a week (in Murie's time) and the boat was hired at £4 10s to £4 15s by a London merchant who also provided the net, boxes and carriage.

The net was rowed round from the shore in a bight; then the two men pulled it ashore by the ends with the boy splashing in the water to drive the bait into the pocket. Murie describes a trip, setting out at three am and working just above Westcliff. By 8.30 am they had made ten hauls (of which the first was a failure because the pocket was inside out) and they put two and a half boxes on the 9.40 am train. Other boats had mustered earlier and gone down as far as Shoebury and the Maplins. In June and July they worked the Swale and all round the Isle of Sheppey.

The last whitebait stowboater, *Saxonia*, was built for Young's by Aldous of Brightlingsea in 1935-6, when she was also the last smack to come from that famous yard. When members of the Young family took her on a holiday cruise to Holland she was recognised and greeted as a stowboater by the fishermen at Zierickzee. After serving as a dredger with Colchester Oystery Fishery she was rigged for sailing in 1977 by the managing director of the fishery, Mr Christopher Kerrison.

The all-the-year-round trade had a setback in 1914, when the merchants and fishermen made an agreement (from which some soon withdrew) to cease fishing in August and September "when whitebait cannot be taken in sufficient numbers to pay wages and expenses", with a penalty of £500 payable to the other signatories for any breach. This seems curious, for today August is a good month, but possibly the idea was to avoid high summer in the times before freezers.

Cecil Osborne is one of the last men in Leigh to remember the old days and ways. Between the wars he was responsible for two bawleys, receiving £20 10s a week, to be split into six shares. They fished sometimes by the Yantlet or up at Hole Haven, or in the low way at the mouth of Hadleigh Ray, but mostly off the end of the pier where there would often be eight bawleys tightly bunched to make the best of the three tidal streams at this point. Without echo sounders or help from the gulls they went where instinct and experience directed, and made the best of what they found there. While Murie gives the second quarter of the flood as the best time, Cecil Osborne insists that the best catches were taken on the ebb. Both agree that night and day were immaterial.

Stowboating for whitebait lasted a little longer than for sprats, the last pair of boats working for Young's till 1965 or 1966. Then the trade was revolutionised not only by echo sounders and by Larsen trawls, but by a third innovation equally fundamental, freezing.

Today it is still a prosperous and vigorous trade carried on chiefly by two firms, Gilsons, and John Bridge who comes of an old fishing family and who epitomises the Leigh philosophy, which differs greatly from that of north Essex. For at Leigh there has always been a questing energy and progressive drive, the lack of which has led to the decline of inshore fishing both at Tollesbury and Brightlingsea. though for some reason a comparable vigour has appeared at West Mersea, till recently devoted only to yachting and oyster cultivation. Perhaps the essence of it is that whereas in north Essex men carried on till the last with old motorised sailing smacks, built by their grandfathers, the Leigh men respected the boat's share and used it for building new craft. The average age of fishing boats in the Colne and Blackwater (other than West Mersea) is perhaps fifty years; at Leigh ten.

John Bridge's grandfather's bawley, the *Happy Home,* is but a family memory; indeed there is hardly an old time bawley to be seen in these waters. The survivors have mostly been adopted as yachts in the conservative and sentimental backwaters of north Essex.* Instead Leigh is full of beamy, powerful, light-draught craft, as shallow as flat irons but well suited to their own waters. Three of these are today the fleet of John Bridge and his partner Bob Osborne, questing after the shoals with their pair trawls and echo sounders and marvelling at the blind fishing of Cecil Osborne's days, when the bawleys optimistically stood and waited in places which today the sounders do not even recommend as worth trying. They have their own sheds and freezer and handle between half a ton a day in hot weather and a ton a day for the London market where bait is still in as keen demand as ever in the restaurants. The price when the old currency went out was about 2s a pound; today it is around 24p to 30p.

It is an attractive survival, even though overshadowed by the ever-present problem of pollution and the continuing threat of industrial development at Maplin. The building of a third London Airport on the sands has been abandoned, but the plan for a tanker port would probably destroy the old fisheries with equal finality.

*At the present time the bawleys *Bona* and *Helen and Violet* are being restored at Brightlingsea and the *Doris* at Tollesbury.

CHAPTER SEVEN

The Flying Shoot

WHEN THE whitebait were driven down to Leigh and the fishermen found it practicable to pursue them, it must have been clear that bigger nets were needed to work from bigger boats in open waters, and, as has been mentioned, the Leighmen adopted the existing stowboat gear as the answer. Though the baiters replaced the long sleeves by a short sweat rag, for spratting long sleeves were, of course, necessary. For a shoal of sprats to hit whitebait gear could be a disaster, as the whole net filled, and Cecil Osborne recalls having to tear away at the wides with a boat hook to make a rent through which a cloud of sprats poured up.

The Leigh men's chief contribution to stowboat technique was their "flying shoot". Instead of laboriously working the baulks round under the bow they would, under favourable conditions, launch the whole gear overboard abaft the starboard rigging*. As soon as the bawley snubbed to her anchor and the handfleets were shackled in, the skipper gave her a hard sheer to port, slipping a hitch on the tiller. The crew then launched the forward ends of the baulks overboard and gave the aft ends a shove to get everything clear. This manoeuvre, which was only attempted with a good tide running, was very spectacular, especially as the spratting

*Murie, describing the flying shoot, says that the "forward templine was passed round the bawley's stern on the port side." In fact the after templine must have been led round the bow. This is one of the instances that shows Murie was not infallible and justifies questioning some of his other statements and diagrams.

bawleys only carried three in crew, and earned the grudging admiration of Tollesbury and Brightlingsea men, who could not attempt it from their "vessels" because of the risk of catching forelint on the rigging set on projecting channels. "Navvy" Mussett, however, declares that it involved a lot of "frap-ups" and torn lints.

The early bawleys inherited from Greenwich and Gravesend a great London street trade. According to Henry Mayhew* three-quarters of all the sprats sold in London (which total he put at four million pounds weight) were taken by coster-mongers, for the street fishmongers considered them, along with winkles and stewed mussels, beneath their dignity, at any rate so long as they could find something more profitable.

The season was reckoned to last ten weeks, starting on Lord Mayor's Day (November 9), which was sometimes called "Sprat Day". The fish were sold at Billingsgate by the "chuck" or "toss", about half a bushel weighing forty to fifty pounds, and retailed by the penny-worth, though there was also some trade in bundles of dried sprats, thirty to a bundle†. In the days

*London Labour and the London Poor, 1864.

†Mayhew was inaccurate; a full bushel weighed about 56lbs. The smacksmen reckoned their tonnage on the basis that two bushels weighed a hundredweight. His coster's preference for stewing sprats sounds curious, but the favourite way of cooking aboard the smacks was to stew them for just four minutes. Smoked sprats also needed a short dip in hot water to make them swell and become soft and palatable.

when a fish diet was becoming "almost as common among the ill-paid classes of London as is a potato diet among the peasants of Ireland" the costers would cry them through the streets — "Oy! Oy! Oy! Now's your time! Fine grizzling sprats! All large and no small!"

One of these costers told Mayhew, "Gentlemen's servants is very fond of them and mechanics comes down such as shoemakers in their leather aprons and sings out 'Here, old sprats, give us two penn-orth.' They're such a relish. I sell more to men than women perhaps but there is little difference. They're best stewed, Sir, I think — if you're fond of sprats — with vinegar and a pick of allspice. That's my opinion, and only yesterday an old cook said I was right. I makes 1s 6d to 2s 6d a day and sometimes rather more on my sprats and sticks to 'em as much as I can. I sell about my 'toss' a day, seldom less. Of course, I can make as many penn'orths of it as I please but there is no custom without one gives middling penn'orths. If a toss costs me 3s I may make 60 penn'orths of it — sometimes 70 or more, and sometimes less than 60."

By the end of the nineteenth century the disappearance of petty dealers, described as "chiefly of Irish extraction", was being blamed as one of the reasons for the trade's difficulties. Smoking was started in the 1880's by an oyster dredgerman, Ted Frost, but it did not come to much and no cannery or pickling yard developed.

Thus while Leigh and Southend had twenty or thirty spratters before 1914, and there was some export trade from Tilbury to Russia during the First World War, barrelled in brine, there was a decline between the wars rather than the boom enjoyed at Brightlingsea. Living memory recalls four boats working from Southend and fifteen from Leigh*, but most of the sprats they caught went across to Kent or up to Gravesend for manure at 30s a ton. This was nothing new, for in earlier times muck barges lay in Sea Reach to receive catches.

When the trade had some value, before 1914, the boats worked in fleets, as in baiting, with one bawley acting as carrier. The others would leave a full sleeve alongside till the carrier came to collect its contents and sometimes a full sleeve would be sold to another bawley in the water and towed across as soon as the bargain was struck.

But the fishery never acquired the romantic, adventurous associations that it enjoyed in north Essex. The Leigh men went to Harwich in summer for shrimping but in winter they seldom left home waters. They did not join the Tollesbury and Brightlingsea fleets in the Wallet, and very seldom visited Brightlingsea to find a buyer. This was probably because they knew "foreigners" would not be welcome, though on one occasion "Navvy" Mussett did introduce a Southender.

He had been fishing in the *Paragon* in company with one of the Thomases in the Southend bawley *Marian* when they both filled in the Middle Deeps in a fog. It was a Friday afternoon and Thomas lamented that now he had caught his 400 bushels he did not know what to do with them over the weekend, for he was against Sabbath-breaking. "Take 'em into

*See appendix.

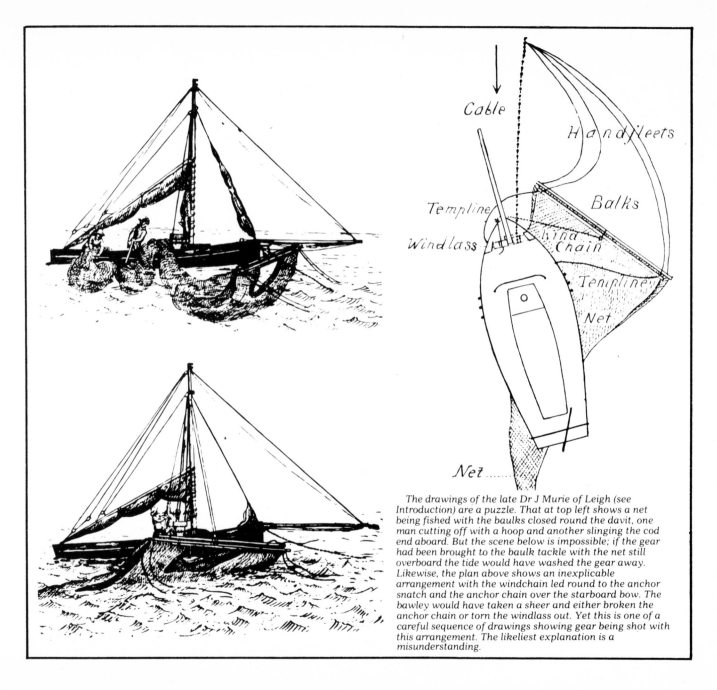

The drawings of the late Dr J Murie of Leigh (see Introduction) are a puzzle. That at top left shows a net being fished with the baulks closed round the davit, one man cutting off with a hoop and another slinging the cod end aboard. But the scene below is impossible; if the gear had been brought to the baulk tackle with the net still overboard the tide would have washed the gear away. Likewise, the plan above shows an inexplicable arrangement with the windchain led round to the anchor snatch and the anchor chain over the starboard bow. The bawley would have taken a sheer and either broken the anchor chain or torn the windlass out. Yet this is one of a careful sequence of drawings showing gear being shot with this arrangement. The likeliest explanation is a misunderstanding.

Latter day motorised bawleys with baulk davits and baulks in rigging. LO32 has her aft dead eye and lanyard wolded, a fog bell on her mast and her windchain rove. The rigging plates, fitted flush on the rails and sheer strake, made possible the "flying shoot".

Brightlingsea," advised "Navvy", but Thomas declared he did not know the way even in clear weather, so as the *Marian* had a small engine and the *Paragon* had not they lashed alongside each other and were soon in the Colne. There they were offered 6d a bushel, but "Navvy" promptly replied that they could get 9d at Tollesbury. This figment of the imagination was partly to spur on the Brightlingsea buyer and partly in case he wanted the *Marian* to tow him home. Going ashore he 'phoned Tollesbury, telling them the Brightlingsea offer was 1s 3d, which raised the Tollesbury bid to 1s 6d. This was enough to extract 2s from the Brightlingsea buyer, at which figure they settled. Thomas was delighted but still faced the problem of finding his way out of this strange place. "Start an hour before high water, steer due south and you'll go over the top of everything till you get to the Blacktail and then you'll know where you are," advised "Navvy". It must have worked, for later when they were again in the south channels they saw a boat pulling over from the bawley fleet towards the *Paragon*, which was easily recognised by her long topmast and brown hull. It was Thomas with a bottle of whisky.

"Navvy" believes this was the first time a Southender had been into Brightlingsea to sell his catch, and the story illustrates the insularity of the two centres.

In view of the inevitable tendency to glamorise and romanticise old ways and other days, perhaps it is as well to say farewell to Leigh with this earthy account of a far-from-flying shoot from A E Copping's immortal *Gotty and the Guv'nor:—*

" 'Eave the lead!" Gotty commanded. The third hand did so.

"Seven fathom!" he announced, as he drew in the line. He threw the lead again. "Seven fathom!" Then again and still again, with these successive readings:

"Seven fathom and a half." "Eight fathom less a quarter." "Eight fathom."

"Leggo!" thundered Gotty, and there was a noisy rush of chain as the mate released the anchor.

The spirit of toil and tumult, having thus descended once more on the *Breadwinner*, tarried awhile with us.

To what precise end the commander and crew were exercising their bodies and tongues so unsparingly, I was not at the moment privileged to learn. I merely saw that they were desperately set on shoving some long netty object into the sea, while the long netty object seemed equally determined not to go. But the final victory lay with brain and muscle, though it would seem that the mutinous thing of meshes indulged at the moment of defeat in one final spasm of misbehaviour. For, immediately after the heavy splash, Gotty's voice arose in panic lamentations:

"She's fast! Foul o' the rudder, ain't she! A nice thing ter 'appen! 'Ere, Jim — the boat-'ook, quick! And wery likely broke 'er templins! Don't be all night, Jim! She's tore — I lay she's tore. Yer know, it's all that young 'un's fault! 'E must 'ave 'ung on too long at that end, istid o' lettin' go. I wish 'e wouldn't shove 'is face in so much; 'e 'inders a lot more than 'e 'elps."

"I wasn't touching it!" came the boy's shrill, indignant protest.

"Then you ought to 'a bin!" roared Gotty, manifestly blind, in his perturbation, to the finer shades of equity.

Jabbing with a boat-hook yielded no relief to a situation that filled the entire ship's company with growing excitement, and presently I beheld Gotty scramble into the dinghy, that he might get at close quarters with what was amiss.

And now I had my second experience of the astonishing swiftness with which, at sea, calm succeeds storm. The net having been prevailed upon to descend to its appointed duties, the crisis was not merely ended, but obliterated. Gotty and the boy were already exchanging friendly ideas about the possibility of rain before the dawn.

"It warn't nothing'," Gotty took his pipe from his mouth to politely explain, when I pressed for details, "only one o' them jumps catched under the rudder. It easy 'appens with the tide runnin' anyways strong ter lu'ard. Yer see," he added, by way of revealing the full significance of recent operations in their entirety, "we're standin' now. Draggin' comes afterwards."

And gradually I pieced together a conception of how we rode there at anchor above a broad stretch of net into which the tide was sweeping unwary whitebait.

"I don't 'ardly look ter catch more than a gallon," Gotty said feelingly, by way of supplement to information of a more general character. "The net's that rotten it ain't fit ter keep crows off a row of peas; only there's a noo 'un comin', and the sooner the better. Don't it stand ter reason," he asked argumentatively, "that yer can't catch a small fish like that — and wonderful quick a whitebait is! — when there's 'oles in the net big enough fer a twenty-pound codfish ter go through!"

It was a little past midnight. Gotty set the alarm to a quarter to three; and, anon, snoring proclaimed slumber.

On being disturbed by what I fondly hoped was a premature demonstration on the part of the clock, I opened my reluctant eyes to unmistakable dawn. When I reached the deck, the net had already been lifted. Its freight of seaweed and little wriggling fishes was being emptied into a tub.

"That net's wusser than I thought," lamented Gotty, as he shook his head over the smallness of the catch.

The mate, the third hand, and the boy got into the dinghy, and rowed away to a belt of sand that figured mistily in the cold grey morning. With another net they "dragged" in shallow water, the boy on shore walking with one end of the supporting line, the other end being fastened to the boat, which the two men rowed. After the warmth of the cabin, this occupation repelled by its suggestion of chilly discomfort.

Seeing me yawn, Gotty prescribed a little more sleep; nor was I reluctant to resume my tenancy of his bunk.

On re-awaking two hours later, I found a fire in the cabin stove, bacon fizzing in the frying-pan, a loaf of bread on the floor and my hospitable skipper ready to put a handful of tea in the kettle.

When the crew came back there was more head-shaking; for they had captured only three quarts of whitebait, six dabs, two eels, and a dog-fish.

Solent cutter off Cowes with stowboat gear. She is "right-handed" and could be one of the imported Essex smacks. But the starboard quarterboard is not cut short to the extent favoured in Essex.

CHAPTER EIGHT

Around the Coast

WHILE STOWBOATING was primarily a Thames Estuary occupation, it was carried on to a less extent on the south coast, in Morecambe Bay and in the Wash, while in the Bristol Channel different but comparable techniques evolved.

Wherever fish were carried by the tide through suitable channels the need must have been felt to fix a net in the path of the shoals, starting with the primitive method, still employed in the Solway, of the fishermen standing in the tide holding the net. There may well have been other local variations unrecorded or unknown to me.

On the South Coast there was quite a sizeable fishery in the Solent, based on the Hamble, Cowes and Portsmouth, stowboating for sprats between October and February. Mr Banks, of Hythe on Southampton Water, owner of the little twenty foot half-deck Solent cutter *Nellie,* built for his grandfather, recalls that she and others of her kind once took part in this trade. Sometimes they went out into Christchurch Bay or the Solent, but usually got all they needed in Southampton Water. About 1890 twenty-two smacks and eighty men were spratting from Hamble alone, including several old Essex smacks such as *Gipsy Queen, Jemima, Welfare* and *Racer.* It thus seems possible the fishery was introduced from Essex and the smacks with it. But it was sufficiently well established in 1883

for Holdsworth to note that: "Vast quantities are caught by the fishermen of Itchen, Cowes and Portsmouth and for the most part landed at Southampton." Thus, whether it was learnt from the same source or not, stowboating was practised in the Solent before it was adopted at Tollesbury.

During the First World War the fisheries were under Government control and declined sharply. Only three spratters were left working in 1920, including the former Bembridge pilot boat *Ariel.* Another cause of decline, as at Leigh, may have been lack of market, for while prices up to 5s a bushel are recorded, when there was a glut there was no alternative to dumping on the village hards for disposal as manure at give-away prices.

At nearby Poole, instead of stowboat gear the boats used fourteen-foot beam trawls with light, small-mesh nets devoid of pockets and with the beam raised about four feet above the top of the heads on iron supports. A record catch of 240 bushels in a day was claimed. The season started in November and lasted three to five months. Prices ranged from 3s a bushel down to 3d or 4d for manure.

At Morecambe it seems that the fishermen made a visit "down south" about 1912 and came back with information about a "hanging net" which they copied and referred to as a "bogie" net. J T Woodhouse was its first and main user. It had a mouth about eighteen feet square and was used for whitebait. A big catch was made in the spring of 1963 following a cold winter, but the method has since died out with the general decline of the fishery.

In the Wash a small net with a triangular mouth was used up the rivers for shrimps and a larger stow net in the estuaries for sprats. This probably approximated to the Essex gear but it borrowed the small local net's name and was also called a trim net. The templines were known as weagle lines. Mr J Castleton, a 75-year-old fisherman of King's Lynn, remembers his father talking of it, but it was not

used in his time and he dates its end around 1912.

In the West Country two variations were used. At Hotwells, near Bristol, a "double trawl" was employed till about 1927. The weighted upper and lower beams were each about thirty feet long and about fifteen feet across at the mouth, made of four triangles of shrimp net. With this gear the bridles did not lead to the chain or cable like handfleets, but to the bow, the net being fished over the stern. Instead of

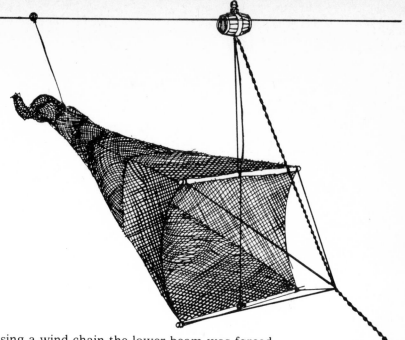

Stowboat net without a stowboat. How it was done at Clevedon and Weston-Super-Mare.

using a wind chain the lower beam was forced down by an iron rod worked by a tackle on the mizzen mast. A small boat lying astern was used to empty the cod ends one after the other, and it is claimed that flat fish were caught ten feet off the bottom.

At Clevedon and Weston-Super-Mare a stownet complete with handfleets was worked without using a smack at all, but hung from a buoy. The baulks were as long as eighteen feet, the upper wood and the lower iron, and the gape was also about eighteen feet. When the gear was cleared the baulks were closed by a line acting as a wind chain. It is difficult to see how "windmills" were avoided in a net left to swing to the tide without the support of templines which, of course, could not be used.

★   ★   ★

There you have it then; an unimportant little human activity, insignificant economically and far less dramatic and romantic than a number of other fisheries. The voyages after cod and herrings which swayed the policies and the fate of nations, were on quite another scale, both as

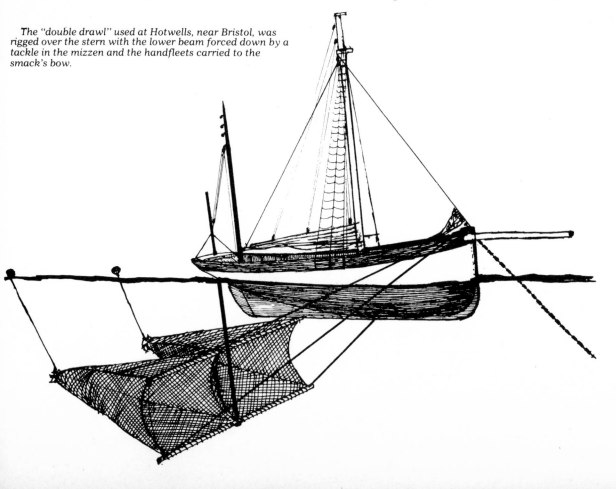

The "double drawl" used at Hotwells, near Bristol, was rigged over the stern with the lower beam forced down by a tackle in the mizzen and the handfleets carried to the smack's bow.

In her last berth. Joe Hume's Waterlily at Tollesbury. She was one of the last smacks to sail to Jersey for new potatoes and kept her stern cabin to the end.

to the areas fished and as to the number and variety of fishermen and fishing craft engaged. Other fisheries besides these deserve to be recorded, and there will be others yet to be invented, for even with scientific and mechanical equipment exerting an increasing influence fishing will continue to be fishing (inshore fishing, at any rate!) until one day, I dare say, the decisions will pass to a man at a computer who will pronounce just how many fish may be killed each day by duly licensed electrocuting circuits — or perhaps, with the exception of those reserved for anglers, all fish will be farmed and there will be none left to be hunted.

Yet it is precisely because of its modest domestic scale that the long story of the stowboaters has fascinated me. It was just one of the many examples of the inventiveness and hardy living that distinguished the old culture — a technique and way of life developed over centuries and like so many more swept away in a decade. Human ingenuity renews and reasserts itself, but now it is directed into electronics and the avoidance of laborious adventure. To that extent the stowboaters will never live again.

Appendix

The following stowboaters are recalled by the contributors to this book. The list is not complete, and several of the smacks belonged at different times to other ports, and were owned and skippered by a number of different individuals. The names in brackets indicate a name particularly associated with the smack, sometimes as owner, sometimes as skipper. Where both owner and skipper are recalled they are shown thus (owner/skipper).

BRIGHTLINGSEA

Ellen CK222 (J Francis, H Heard.)
Kingfisher (Knight/Fisher.)
Guide SM284 (T Poole.)
Wonder CK40 (G Carter.)
Verona CK442 (Death, H Frost.)
Claude CK285 (G Francis.)
Olive CK102 (J Francis/W Godfrey.)
Iris Mary CK105 (J Francis, J Heard.)
Helen and Violet CK17 (D Leavett.)
Favourite (R Brand.)
Sunbeam CK328 (W Gunn/B Steady.)
T.C.H.J. (*Foxhound*) (J Goodwin.)
Masonic (J Cook.)
Magnolia (Death.)
Boy Kenneth CK8 (Paul/C Gunn.)
Advent (formerly *Wave* of Wivenhoe) (F Goodwin.)
Marion (British Fish Canners/S Bishop.)
Francois (British Fish Canners/R. Fisher.)
Blanche CK302 (A Cranfield/S Bishop.)

WIVENHOE & ROWHEDGE

Mary (D. Welham.)
Ellen CK321 (R. Cranfield.)

Volunteer CK21 (E Green.)
Elise CK299 (J Green.)
Christine CK35 (North Sea Canners/CF Woodward.)
Xanthe CK103 (Cranfield.)
Alice Matilda (North Sea Canners/S Green.)
William & Eliza (*Tally*) (G Glazier/C & H Gunn, formerly at Tollesbury owned by Mr Tally Gager.)
Jane CK355 (Garwood.)
Neva.

MERSEA

Priscilla (R Stoker/C Brand.)
George & Alice.

TOLLESBURY

Charlotte Ellen CK257 (D Heard.)
Paragon.
Express CK321.
Volante CK15 (D Heard.)
Bertha (B Leavett.)
Bluebell CK104 (L Heard.)
Maria CK21.
Emma CK369.
My Alice CK348 (L Heard.)
My Kate CK25 (Sid Lewis.)
Rosena CK65 (E Heard.)
Thistle CK324.
Alpha CK180 (B Howe.)
Sallie MN39.
Shamrock CK200.
William & Emily (*Odd Times*) CK112 (W Mussett.)
S.W.H. CK492 (T Miles.)
A.D.C. CK431 (R Frost.)
A.B.C.
Mollie.

A.E.F.A. CK114.
Gladys CK77 (A Lewis.)
Alberta CK318 (S Heard.)
Betsan MN41 (A Lewis.)

Bawleys which were stowboating during the last forty years include:

SOUTHEND

Irene LO8 (W Thomas.)
May LO180 (W Thomas.)
Marian LO182 (W Thomas.)
Souvenir LO5 (S Thomas.)

LEIGH

Ellen LO7 (W Turnnidge.)
Iris LO245 (R Turnnidge.)
Verona LO253 (A Turnnidge.)
Olive LO225 (S Cotgrove.)
Elsie Mildred LO21 (A Dolby.)
Vera LO114 (A Kirby.)
Onward LO181 (S Oliver.)
Osprey LO269 (G Dolby.)
Bona LO99.
Enterprise LO58 (A Myall.)
Maud LO2 (E Frost.)
Doris LO284 (W King.)
Alice Matilda LO145 (W Young.)
Erato LO204 (C Osborne.)
Emma Rebecca (C Osborne.)
In addition to the above, which were sometimes spratters, W Young's *Prima Donna* and *Saxonia* were stowboating exclusively for whitebait.

Glossary

Aforehead. Position of baulks slung across smack's stem from baulk davit.

Barnacle strop. The fixture on the upper baulk through which the wind chain passed. (Presumably because it was fastened snug on the baulk.)

Baulks. Beams to spread top and bottom of net mouth.

Baulk davit. Wooden crane rigged over starboard bow for wind chain to work over a sheave in its outer end. (Probably from proper name David, which old form was used to the end by fishermen in pronunciation and spelling.)

Baulk tackle. Tackle rigged from masthead for lifting baulks. Usually a single rope through a block with four-part purchase on the hauling end.

Bawley. Type of cutter-rigged fishing vessel developed at Leigh and in the Medway, distinguished by square transom stern and boomless main sail. Often thought to be a corruption of boilerboat, from the cauldrons, used in their principal trade of shrimping, but the boats were possibly so named before they fitted boilers. Alternative theories derive the name from boomless boat (the belief of John Cann, of Harwich, their best builder) and from St Bartholomew and a riverside parish (cf. peterboats).

Beckets. Device for securing loose ropes or spars, usually a short lanyard spliced in an eyebolt.

Bogie nets. Stow nets used at Morecambe, Lancashire.

Channels. Projections on the smack's side round which the shroud chains were led, giving, a wider spread to the rigging. (Lit chainwales.)

Chip ropes. The ropes along the baulks to which the forelint was laced.

Chocker pole (or chock staff). Short topmast set up in winter, partly for appearance, but occasionally a small topsail was set on it.

Chuck. Syn for toss (q.v.)

Cod. A rough measure of sprats, about four and a half bushels. Presumably because it was taken in the cod end of the net.

Cod end. The tail of the net, remote from the mouth, in which fish were caught. From the trawlermen's usage for the end of the net in which cod finished up.

Culching. Dredging shell, which was re-laid on oyster layings to receive the spat.

Cutch. Protective dressing made from oak bark.

Cutting-in. Literally, cutting off cods of fish in the sleeves, and hence referring to getting the net in.

Docanoes. Phonetic corruption of docking hose.

Docking hose. The after section of net, into which a section of fish was slid to be shaken in the water (or docked) to get rid of smig and fry, and retain the sprats, as by sifting. Oystermen speak of docking a dredge by shaking it in the water to clear it of mud.

Dog. Iron claw with fingers to grip a link of chain.

Enter (or entry). The second section of net, by which the catch entered the sleeves.

Fennel. Leigh term for up and downs (q.v.)

Five fingers. Fishermen's name for star fish, dredged for manure.

Flasket. Flat basket for fish carrying. At Leigh sometimes called a sheller (shallow).

Forelint. The first, or forward, section of net.

Fry. Young, undersize fish.

Garping strop. Short rope on baulk davit, led round upper baulk and belayed to a cleat to permit lower baulk to be temporarily eased to check that it was clear to drop. (By allowing the baulks to gape or permit a gap.)

Girdlines. Lines with which the sleeves were girdled to secure them to the smack. Chain girdlines were of wolded chain with rope tails. Thimble girdlines were all rope with a thimble in one end, the other end being passed through the thimble so that the girdline could be drawn tight like a snare.

Gorings. Triangular panels of net at the hundreds (q.v.)

Handfleets. The four ropes controlling the ends of the two baulks by connection to the stringer. (Presumably because they were "fleeted" on deck — that is laid out by hand, while other gear was taken to the windlass.)

Hemlets. Gravesend name for handfleets (q.v.)

Hip ropes. Tollesbury alternative for templines (q.v.) While the fixings were perhaps on the shoulders rather than the hips of the smack the sense is probably as a pair of braces supports the trousers round the hips.

Hoop. Tool used as alternative for mingle (q.v.) for cutting off fish in the sleeves.

Hundreds, The. Sections of the net at each end of the baulks. Eight sections, each of twelve meshes, made ninety-six or a round hundred. Sometimes separate triangular panels, also called gorings.

In irons. Description of a vessel head to wind, in which position she loses steerage way and is powerless.

Jump holes. Semi-circular openings cut in the net behind the centre of both baulks to allow the smack's stem to jump in a sea without damaging the net.

Knightheads. Belaying posts on each side of the foredeck.

Larsen fishing. Mid-water trawling, using otterboards, which replaced stowboating. (From its Scandinavian inventor.)

Left-handed smack. Smack with bowsprit to port and anchor snatch to starboard, the style down channel from Shoreham westwards.

Mid-water trawling. See Larsen fishing.

Mingle. Tool for cutting off fish in the sleeves.

Parcelling. Wrapping a rope, wire or chain in protective canvas which was then served (q.v.)

Peak. The top corner of a gaff mainsail. Rucking the peak meant lowering the gaff on the peak halyard, also called scandalising the sail.

Peter boat. Small, double-ended Thames Estuary fishing boat used before the evolution of the bawley. Possibly a reference to the fisherman apostle, or some riverside parish dedicated to him.

Pinion. Rope from after sleeve, led to the tonking post. By the amount of slack and the weight on the rope it could be judged if there were fish in the sleeves.

Putting-to. Getting out the gear for fishing.

Quarterboards. See Washboards.

Right-handed smack. Smack with bowsprit to starboard and anchor snatch to port. The East Coast style.

Scuttle hatch. Small hatch, about two feet square, fitted abaft main hold hatch for sprat loading.

Serving. Protecting rope, wire or parcelled chain by wrapping spunyarn round it.

Shading. Testing and sampling the catch.

Sheller. See Flasket.

Skiff. In spratting, not a light-weight cockleshell, but a heavy clinker-built boat with grown floors and frames, up to eighteen feet long and seven feet beam, used for landing catches. In the early and the final years stowboaters used Hythe Quay, Colchester, but generally everything had to be boated ashore in skiffs.

Sleeper. Toggle shackled to wind chain about five and a half fathoms from lower baulk so that it took the weight of the slack chain on the barnacle strop and prevented it surging through the strop as the smack pitched. This allowed the crew to sleep undisturbed.

Sleeves. Circular tunnels of net in which the catch was secured.

Smig. Undersize fish.

Snatch, anchor. The fairlead on the stem through which the anchor chain led to the windlass.

Sniff. Undersize fish, rubbish. See also Smig and Fry.

Stall boat. Old name for stowboat (q.v.) (From stall, meaning fixed.)

Stovet. Harwich pronunciation of stowboat.

Stowboat. Name for boat fishing with nets slung below her from anchor cable. (Perhaps because sails were stowed, but reason for change from stallboat (q.v.) is obscure.)

Stringer. Short length of chain or wire connecting handfleets to anchor chain or cable, or at Gravesend sometimes long chain connecting handfleets to anchor.

Sugaring. Arranging the catch to best advantage for market.

Sweat rag. Short net end used by whitebaiters instead of long sleeves use by spratters.

Swolding. See Wolding.

Tailings. Lengths of rope, eye-spliced into chain shackles and short-spliced into cable wormings.

Templines. The vertical ropes by which the upper baulk was suspended from the foredeck of the smack, one on each side. Possibly from "tempering lines", since they adjusted the fishing depth; the word was sometimes pronounced "temperin's". See also hip ropes.

Thimble. Metal eye spliced into rope or sewn into sail.

Thole pins. Oak pins shipped in holes in the rail for belaying ropes, positioning a trawl warp or occasionally as a bearing for an oar. Thus, thole holes in which washboard stanchions were shipped.

Thrumming. Jamming of fish or other matter in the meshes, usually in the forelint and enter. Most cottages had thrum mats made from old clothes cut up into thrums. Strips of clothing pushed through a hessian backing.

Tide, making. Tide increasing from neaps to springs. The reverse process was called taking off.

Timber nogging. The post socketing in the stern bench to which the pinion was belayed. (Nogging pieces were short lengths of stud put in between the uprights of a half-timber building to stiffen it before the brick nogging for filling was put in.) At Tollesbury called tonking post.

Tonking post. See timber nogging.

Toss. Billingsgate sprat measure stated to have been about half a bushel, weighing forty to fifty pounds, but in fact a full bushel weighed about fifty-six pounds.

Trim nets. Stow nets used in the Wash.

Up and downs. Vertical ropes between ends of baulks to take weight of lower baulk when wind chain was eased away.

Washboards. Boards shipping in bulwarks on each quarter for protection, specially in loaded trim. Sometimes called quarterboards.

Weagle lines. King's Lynn name for templines. Possibly because they used to wiggle so vigorously in a strong tide that "puddings" of old rope were put on them to stop them beating against the smack's sides.

Well boats. Boat with section sealed off by water-tight bulkheads, with sea water circulating in it.

Wend. Essex name for tacking, that is sailing the smack round through the wind from one tack to the other.

Wides. Forelint (q.v.)

Wind chain. Chain by which baulks were raised or wound up on the anchor windlass. It was often called wink chain and may derive from big smack practice of handing it on a trawl winch, or "dandy wink".

Windmill (or windmiller). Accidental crossing of the baulks.

Wobbling. See Wolding.

Wolding. Swaddling in old rope against chafe. Also called wobbling or swolding.

Worming. Laying a rope in the lay of another rope.

Yawling. Young herring. (Perhaps from Norfolk pronunciation of yearling.)